$L \cdot O \cdot S \cdot T$
FRIENDSHIPS

BY DONALD WINDHAM

Novels
The Dog Star
The Hero Continues
Two People
Tanaquil
Stone in the Hourglass
(limited edition)

Short Stories
The Warm Country

Autobiography
Emblems of Conduct

Drama
You Touched Me
(with Tennessee Williams)

EDITED BY DONALD WINDHAM

E. M. Forster's Letters
to Donald Windham
(limited edition)

Tennessee Williams' Letters
to Donald Windham, 1940–1965

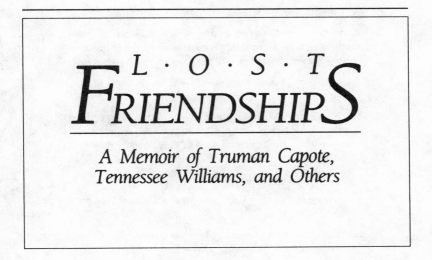

L·O·S·T
FRIENDSHIPS

A Memoir of Truman Capote,
Tennessee Williams, and Others

DONALD WINDHAM

PARAGON HOUSE
NEW YORK

First paperback edition, 1989

Published in the United States by

Paragon House Publishers
90 Fifth Avenue
New York, NY 10011

Copyright © 1983, 1985, 1987 by Donald Windham

Reprinted by arrangement with William Morrow &
Company, Inc.

Most of the material appearing in this book has been printed
privately by Sandy Campbell in Italy in two volumes:
Footnote to a Friendship and *As If . . . : A Personal View of
Tennessee Williams.*

Library of Congress Cataloging-in-Publication Data
Windham, Donald.
Lost friendships : a memoir of Truman Capote, Tennessee
Williams, and others / Donald Windham. — 1st pbk. ed.
p.   cm.
Reprint. 1st ed. Originally published: New York : Morrow,
c1987.
ISBN 1-55778-240-7
1. Windham, Donald—Friends and associates. 2. Capote,
Truman, 1924- —Biography. 3. Williams, Tennessee,
1911- —Biography. 4. Authors, American—20th
century—Biography. I. Title.
[PS3573.I5Z473   1989]
818′.5403—dc20
[B]   89-31493   CIP

Manufactured in the United States of America

CONTENTS

ILLUSTRATIONS

The following photographs may be found between pages 97 and 104.

Truman and Don, Piazza San Marco, July 1948

Don and Sandy, Florence, April 1948
(Photograph by Tennessee Williams)

Gore, Truman and Tennessee, New York, October 1948
(Photograph by Jo Healy)

Tennessee in his salad days, Provincetown

Monty, New York, 1948
(Photograph by Karl Bissinger)

André Gide, Greek Theater, Taormina, April 1950

*Tennessee with Frank Merlo, Donald Windham, Maria
Britneva and Sandy Campbell, New York, December 1948*

Tennessee, Italy, June 1948

*Truman: "He liked people and wanted to be liked;
he charmed."*
(Photograph by Fred Melton)

The following photographs may be found between pages 201 and 208.

Tennessee, Biloxi, 1946

Tennessee (in the early 1940s), with friends on Captain Jack's
Wharf in Provincetown, where he met Kip

Tennessee on the beach, Provincetown, 1941

Tennessee, Marlon Brando and Jo Healy, 1947

Tennessee in the Dance Index office, New York, 1943

Tennessee, Piazza di Santa Maria in Trastevere, Rome, May
1948

"With love from Charlie J. Fatburger and
friend," postcard from Spain, August 1961

Truman and Sandy on the Kansas border, October 1964
(Photograph by Alvin Dewey)

Tennessee and Don in Jack Dempsey's Bar, June 1944

Tennessee and Don in Rome, 1948

FOREWOR D

Both Tennessee Williams and Truman Capote were alive when the first of these two memoirs was written. "Footnote to a Friendship" was undertaken, at least in part, in an effort to reach them. Tennessee died while the limited edition was at the printers in 1983. I never learned whether Truman read it. And he, too, died while I was writing "As if. . . ."

Neither of the stories these memoirs tell has the ending I would have liked. Their denouements are unwanted données. But since they were given to me, together with all that went before, and are not merely personal and peculiar, but typical of their place and time, I have tried to set them down as accurately and objectively as their closeness will allow.

Fortunately, the ends of these stories are the smallest parts of them. Tennessee and I were friends for more than three decades, beginning in 1940, before his success; and my friendship with Truman dated from 1948, the first year of his. This friendliness was not three-way. Truman and Tennessee never became close, despite Truman's wishing it. Our involvements were separate. Indeed, they drew together only toward their catastrophic ends, at the close of the 1970s.

Full-length biographies of Truman and Tennessee are now being written, but my perspective of them is different from that of the biographers. I view them looking forward; the biographers view them looking back. I cannot but see the unlikeliness of what Tennessee and Truman became in the light of what they were. The biographers, deducing what they were in the light of what they became, miss the guideposts furnished by the improbable turns and contradictions their lives took and which, with luck, point toward the truth.

In character, Truman and Tennessee were very different. Perhaps the oddest element of their histories is that at the ends of their lives they shared one unlikely trait: as highly rewarded with celebrity and money as they were, each considered himself underappreciated and undercompensated, badly treated by public and critics, a personal example of the failure of America to value and recompense its artists.

But that is getting ahead of my stories.

"*. . . youth, strength, genius, thoughts, achievements, simple hearts—all die . . . No matter.*"

—Joseph Conrad, "Youth"

FOOTNOTE TO·A FRIENDSHIP

A Memoir of
Truman Capote and Others

230 Central Pk. South
New York, N.Y.

2 August 1978

Dear Don and Sandy —

Having wonderful time.
Wish you were here. No,
I wouldn't wish that on
my best friends, which
you are. Love

Trina

The letter from Elisabeth Van Rysselberghe on page 45 is printed with the permission of Catherine Gide. The letter from Jo Healy, on pages 109–110 and the photograph on page 99 are printed with the permission of Erin Clermont.

"Some people might have made a book out of it; but the story I am going to tell is one which it took all my strength to live and over which I spent all my virtue."

—André Gide, *Strait Is the Gate*

ONE

"Be bold. Be bold. Be not too bold."

—Isak Dinesen, "On Mottoes of My
Life"

From my journal: "Tuesday, July 18, 1978. At breakfast I see in the paper that Truman is on the Stanley Siegel show at 9 A.M.—and there he is, in the same shirt I left him in Sunday afternoon, saying he hasn't been to bed for 48 hours, midway drunk of the stages I saw him in, looking as though he'd fall asleep any minute, calling forth pity but also despair; one new note—he has now latched on to classifying himself with Monty and Marilyn Monroe and announced that he would probably kill himself, like them, by accident."

· 1 ·

T he first draft of this memoir was begun in 1977, after the publication of *Tennessee Williams' Letters to Donald Windham, 1940–1965*, when Truman Capote gave me the right to publish a book of his letters to me. This second book was not to be a copy of the first. Capote's letters were slighter in content and as writing than Williams', except for the best ones. Including these in a reminiscence, I hoped to make "a nougat in which the almonds are good."*

I began my first draft with the observation that it was emblematic of our friendship that we met in Italy, even though both Capote and I lived in New York. This still strikes me as the best springboard for what is to follow. However, my "nougat" in this version cannot have the flavor and texture I hoped for then. Leaving aside the question of the "almonds," I have in the meantime lost many of my sweeteners. Cupboards that were full then are empty now. Others contain surprise ingredients I never expected to have. Still, even though almost everything else has changed in the intervening years, the significance of that initial observation seems to me to remain the same.

Capote and I not only both lived in Manhattan in 1948 but,

*André Gide, *Journals*, November 7, 1909

along with hundreds of other people, both frequented Leo Lerman's Sunday evening open house. Nevertheless, although I had once seen him arriving there as I was leaving, we had never spoken. We had never met anywhere else. And in the thirty-five years since our friendship began we have never been invited to the same party in New York.

The year before our meeting an event occurred which, indirectly, brought it about. In October 1947, Cyril Connolly published a story of mine, "Single Harvest," in the American issue of *Horizon*. In his editor's introduction to the number, speaking of literature's losing battle against the "Book Business" in the United States, he wrote:

The hunt for young authors who, while maintaining a prestige value (with a role for Ingrid Bergman), may yet somehow win the coveted jack-pot, is feverish and incessant. Last year's authors (most of the names that have just reached England) are pushed aside and this year's—the novelist Jean Stafford, her poet husband Robert Lowell or the dark horse, Truman Capote—are inevitably mentioned. They may be quite unread, but their names, like a new issue on the market, are constantly on the lips of those in the know. "Get Capote"—at this minute the words are resounding on many a sixtieth floor, and "get him" of course means make him and break him, smother him with laurels and then vent on him the obscure hatred which is inherent in the notion of another's superiority.

To which a footnote added:

For this reason we have tried to avoid literary prize-givings in this number and to present a cross-section of a living antheap, not a case of mounted butterflies fast-fading and wrongly named.*

Truman's reaction to his having no contribution in the issue was displeasure. It was not in his nature to like being left out, whether of a prize-giving or of a cross section. He said at a

---

*The poetry in the issue was by W. H. Auden, Marianne Moore, Wallace Stevens and E. E. Cummings, all well known; the fiction by John Berryman, Ralph Ellison and me, all obscure.

cocktail party: "If you're going to have an American issue at all, what's the point of including a writer like Donald Windham, who *absolutely nobody* ever heard of?" Fred Melton, with whom I had come to New York from Georgia eight years before, was present and replied: "I've heard of him and he's just as good a writer as you are."

Truman was intrigued. "Don Windham inspires loyalty in people," he said to Sandy Campbell when they met in Paris the following June.

In 1948, Melton and I had not been living together for six years. He was long married and the father of two children. Five years before, I had met Campbell, a freshman at Princeton. After he went from college into the army and was discharged, we started living together in a top-floor walk-up on Madison Avenue. Our trip to Europe in 1948 was our first, as Truman's was his.

Truman not only related the incident with Melton to Sandy, he repeated it to me a couple of weeks later when he arrived in Venice, where Sandy had told him I was. Melton's defense had made me a winner, or at least a dark horse, in his eyes. Unfortunately, he was the only person in the American publishing world in whose eyes I was any such thing.

The publishing world is what I was aware of Capote's being in. We were both writers. Still, although I was twenty-seven and he was only twenty-three, he was in the publishing world and I was not. A play I had written with Tennessee Williams had been produced on Broadway, but during the seven years I had been submitting fiction to American magazines I had accumulated eighty rejections of my handful of stories. I achieved near misses. More than once I was sent a letter from an editor informing me that a story of mine had been accepted, and then the story was returned with a note saying the final decision had been in the negative.* Editors weighed the idea of publishing me but always found some element missing, and I didn't know how to tip the scales in the opposite direction.

On the other hand, even without believing Capote's assertion that he had three of his first stories all accepted in the same

*This happened with *Partisan Review,* for example.

morning's mail when he was seventeen, it is easy to say that his situation was very different from mine. His fiction had appeared in *Story*, the *Atlantic, Harper's, Mademoiselle,* and *Harper's Bazaar.* He had received an O. Henry short-story award in 1946 and was about to receive another. For two summers he had been at Yaddo and become friends with a number of writers who ended up on the staffs of magazines and publishing houses. Random House had just published his first novel, *Other Voices, Other Rooms,* with the kind of fanfare that usually attends the appearance of a movie star in a small town. Added to this, his natural instinct, nurtured by his physically vulnerable personality, was to sell himself, and he had developed an exuberant charm which, with rare exceptions, won anyone he set out to win.

He won Sandy immediately. They met at a cocktail party when Sandy, an actor, was on his way from Venice to the States to look for an acting job for the fall. Before leaving, Truman invited Sandy to go out with him that evening. When he said that he couldn't because he had a ticket for the opera, Truman exclaimed: "Heavens! I never start before eleven-thirty." They made a date to meet at Le Boeuf sur le Toit. After a drink, escaping the admirers who pursued him, Truman whisked Sandy off to Mon Jardin and La Vie en Rose to show him the boys dancing together, the drag shows, and to regale him with stories of his new friendships with André Gide (whom Sandy and I had met in the spring and Sandy had visited that day) and Jean Cocteau, of his going to bed with Albert Camus, of his being photographed by Cecil Beaton, and to hint that, if he wanted to, he could tell in which beds Montgomery Clift had done what in Paris the year before—a mixture of fact and fiction which (and this needs to be said if our friendship with Truman is to be understood at all) we were from the beginning aware of as being such, even if we were frequently unaware which stories were fiction and which fact.

Truman and Sandy "did" Paris the next two nights. On the first they ate together with, as Sandy wrote, "a nice boy from Arkansas who's only been queer a month." On the second Sandy invited Truman to the showing at the MGM screening room of *The Search* which, through Clift, he had arranged for Arletty, whom we had also met that spring.

From Sandy's letter: "Arletty loved Monty and the movie and overstayed her dinner date to see an hour and ten minutes of it. She would say *il est très beau, très beau et gentil* and carried on in much her same manner. And Truman went too and said that it was the first time he had cried since *Dark Victory*."

Ten days later, on the Fourth of July, Truman and the boy from Arkansas arrived in Venice. We encountered each other that evening in Piazza San Marco. Before our parting, I asked the two of them to lunch the next day at the house where I was staying. We began to eat together and Truman and I continued to when, after a few days, the boy from Arkansas departed on his motorcycle.

I was staying on the Grand Canal in a nineteenth-century building with the Firbankian name of the Palazzetto di Madam Stern. Buffie Johnson, a painter and friend of mine, as well as of Tennessee Williams', Fritz Bultman's, etc., from New York, had been lent the whole top floor. When Sandy left Venice I had moved to a small, cheap room beneath the roof of the hotel where we were living and was concentrating on finishing a novel. Shortly afterward, I ran into the newly arrived Buffie, sashaying across Piazza San Marco arm in arm with Peggy Guggenheim. On learning where I was staying, Buffie, smiling from beneath a large white hat trimmed with pink feathers, pouted that it was "ve-ry fool-ish" for me to be paying any rent when she had more space than she knew what to do with and offered me a small room to sleep in, a large one to work in and a bath of my own. I moved in at the end of the week and the setup worked very well in the days before Truman's arrival, mainly because Buffie departed for Rome the morning I came from the hotel. But when she returned, a few days after the boy from Arkansas left, the situation became impossible.

I wanted to work. Buffie wanted a *cavalier servent*. I was asked to carry her portfolio, to accompany her to the Biennale, to attend her on shopping trips.* When I slipped away to a lunch with Truman and, like an erring husband, brought back a bunch of flowers on my return to work, I was sent to the attic to

*Once, she asked me to walk her to the consulate to find out why they had phoned her. They had phoned her to find out why she had phoned them.

search out an appropriate vase, even though she had a dozen vases in her rooms, "because flowers are ve-ry par-tic-u-lar about the vases they are in." I was ripe for departure when Truman, who wanted to finish two stories before he returned to New York in August, suggested that I accompany him to a small town on Lago di Garda he had been told about.

Our departure, however, was dramatically delayed. After the attempted assassination of the Communist leader Togliatti in Rome on the morning we were planning to leave, Venice, a Communist stronghold, was cut off from the rest of Italy by a general strike. No boats arrived or left. No gondolas appeared. No newspapers were published. All shops were closed and the shutters over the entrances of the hotels pulled halfway down. No one knew how long the situation might last. But after three days, on a grim morning of pouring rain, we made our escape. Truman, when I telephoned his hotel at nine, said that the strike was supposed to be over but that San Marco was lined all around the arcades with soldiers, armed with guns and clubs, and that the square itself was full of men who were standing with umbrellas in their hands and rushing the soldiers in attempts to smash the windows of the shops that had opened.

I thought he was exaggerating, but his description was corroborated by another American who was also in Venice and trying to leave. He and Truman arrived at the palazzetto an hour later in a gondola. I added my luggage to theirs and we made our way, past a floating drowned cat, down the Grand Canal to Piazzale Roma. At noon, Truman and I caught a bus for Peschiera. The bus trip, also, was dramatic. The vehicle was repeatedly stopped and searched at army barricades where there were mazes of tanks and machine guns—while Truman entertained me with the running monologue of a used-car dealer's wife from the Midwest ("though I was born in Selma, Alabama, you understand") who was appalled by the foreign goings-on. The drama ended at Verona. In the late afternoon, beneath lifting clouds, we alighted at Peschiera where, learning that the connecting bus was not due for an hour, we took a taxi and arrived, together with clear skies and a rainbow sunset, at a serene and all but deserted Sirmione.

Lago di Garda that year was, truly, a sleeping beauty, not yet awakened by the postwar renewal of tourism. We each had a room with a view of the lake and stayed alone until lunch, working. Then we met to eat and talk. Truman was an inveterate storyteller, and neither one of us lacked subjects for conversation. Even that first evening in Piazza San Marco we stayed up talking after the boy from Arkansas retired. What did we talk about? Not writing. And not Italy. To Truman, traveling was a way of isolation from his social life in New York, but at that time he was not interested in the place where he was. For him, Venice was Harry's Bar. Once, I coaxed him to the Lido, where he rented a cabana and lay on a lounge chair in front of the Excelsior while I walked to the beach the local people frequented. And once, just once, I persuaded him to have a drink not at Harry's Bar but at the small outdoor café in a court off San Marco where I had gone before his arrival. As at Harry's, he ordered a martini. Despite my advocacy of the place, I had to admit that it tasted peculiar. "Ask the bartender what goes into a martini," Truman suggested drily. To my question the answer was: "One third gin, one third vermouth, one third cognac, and a twist of lemon peel."

What we talked about, more or less, was the cognac in our martinis. The unlikely ingredients of everyday life. Gossip—and almost always about people one or the other of us liked. For Truman, although amusing, was not, as his post-TV-talk-show reputation was to label him, vicious. When Sandy, on his return to New York, told Carson McCullers, an old friend of Truman's, that he had met and liked Truman, both Carson and her mother, at first guardedly, and then openly, expressed their dislike of him. He had betrayed her, they said emotionally, by poaching on her subject matter in "A Tree of Night," a story he had published in 1945 when their friendship was just starting and Carson had comfortably considered Truman a disciple and not a too successful rival. Neither of them, they added, had read or intended to read his novel. But Truman spoke to me with equal friendliness of Carson, her mother and her sister, Rita Smith, the fiction editor of *Mademoiselle,* which published his stories. His desire in conversation, as later in his letters, was to be liked, not to put down. His strongest stricture of Carson was "if you criticize her she'll hate you," not an exceptional remark about a writer. He did tell me, with humor, of his last encounter with Carson's mother. "She answered the phone when I called Nyack before I left New York. I said I'd just called to say good-bye because I was going to Europe. And she said goodbye and hung up."

Earlier, in London, Sandy had met Gore Vidal and found him obsessed with Truman and his success. Gore, who two years earlier had been *the* young American author with *his* first novel, *Williwaw,* talked about Truman continually, putting him down, insisting that Truman had never met Gide, Cocteau, etc. In Sirmione, Truman was neither hostile to Gore nor interested in him; and since I didn't know him or his work at the time, only that Tennessee liked him, our conversation about him did not go beyond that.

There were plenty of people Truman was interested in. Every mail brought him piles of letters. He would read me bits of them and launch out into stories about the writers. In the way that people who really have something to say really listen (which was true of him then), Truman, who really liked to be liked, really liked people. I didn't see it at the time, but in the following years I realized that one of the reasons I liked him was that his desire to be liked was in itself likable. This desire often led him into exaggerations and fantasies designed to make himself appear what he considered enviable and therefore, in his eyes, attractive. Given the circumstances, this seemed to me unnecessary; but I found the impulse behind such a need sympathetic. I didn't want to call his bluff and lessen his enjoyment if he could use me as a mirror in his efforts to see himself as he dreamed of being. Our desires were sufficiently different for the things he wanted to be envied for not to be things that would make me envy him. Later, when he was living with Jack Dunphy, nine years Truman's senior, Jack seemed to me complicated in his attitude toward Truman, admiring but strictly censorious of his embroiderings on reality. One spring when the three of us were in Taormina, Jack would say: "The reason Truman likes Donnie is that when he tells him 'one hundred mammoth night-flying moths lit on the window screen in my room last night,' Donnie accepts it as the gospel truth." I didn't. But neither did I feel any need to reply: "For God's sake, Truman, why do you have to lie all the time?"

In New York, in the fifties and sixties, Truman would ask me to go with him to Fifty-seventh Street to buy a Jaguar XKE, wanting a witness to the impression he made on the salesman when he casually announced he would pay cash. Or he would lead me into a gallery to be a spectator, through whom he could see himself as on a movie screen, when he nonchalantly muttered: "I'll take that Fantin-Latour on the wall; would you send it to this address?" If I was surprised by how earnestly he played the game for himself, I nevertheless took pleasure in his pleasure.

As soon as I knew Truman I was impressed by his generosity, material as well as emotional. This perhaps sprang from his desire to be liked, but it also sprang from his pleasure in spending money, the more the better. His joy in the place and the object that was the most expensive reminded me of a sentence in Thomas Raucat's *The Honorable Picnic*: "In our country everything is imitated so well and in so many different ways that there is only one means to determine the genuine: it is that which costs the most."

When, in Venice, after our martinis at Harry's Bar, Truman wanted night after night to eat there, he repeatedly insisted that he would like to pay for me. Once or twice I let him, out of necessity. Truman was not rich then, but I was on shakier financial grounds. I had come to Italy in early spring with only a few hundred dollars to my name and the end of my money was in sight. For ten years, since I was in my teens, I had worked at a wide range of jobs, factory hand, counterman, office clerk. A year and a half before I had quit my last job, editing *Dance Index* for Lincoln Kirstein. I was living on the money I had made from the play Tennessee and I had written together, *You Touched Me,* which had had a brief run on Broadway a year earlier, with Montgomery Clift in the cast. My goal was to finish a novel, but I was a slow worker.

It is hard to realize today on how little money we enjoyed

ourselves in Italy in 1948 and 1950. The lira hovered around 600 to the dollar. The martinis at Harry's Bar were 150 lire. Dinner was proportionately reasonable. But dinner at the Angelo, where I ate before Truman's arrival—and which was millionairess Peggy Guggenheim's habitual restaurant—was 450 lire for soup or pasta, meat, salad, bread and a *quartino* of wine. Our rooms at the Albergo Catullo in Sirmione cost less than five dollars a day each, full pensione. Even so, I was spending more than I had been spending, and more than I spent later when I was on my own again.

The two hotels open in Sirmione that early postwar summer held perhaps two dozen guests. The only other Americans were Robert Penn Warren and his wife, Cinina, staying, as we were, at the cheaper of the two. The town was a good place to work, especially by Truman's standards. It isolated him not only from his New York social life but also from the ordinary life of the country he was in. In this respect it resembled most of the places he was to choose to hole up in and work during the coming years. Nevertheless, being in Sirmione with Truman was for me a little like being in Venice with Buffie. I wanted the added isolation of being on my own in the midst of everyday Italian life; and, although Truman had none of Buffie's demanding impositions, being with him separated me from Italy.

It was no more possible to get Truman into an ordinary café in Sirmione than it was in Venice. Each evening we drank martinis before dinner at the other, more elegant, hotel. Once we picked up two proper, teenaged Italian girls from Milano and danced with them for an hour. But on the street with Truman it was impossible to blend into Italian life. His appearance was impish, not gamin as in those early photographs, which do not resemble him as he looked in the flesh but are the result of his chameleon ability to turn himself before the camera into his dream image. However, his defense in person was never camouflage; it was always boldness. Once, on a New York street, when he was telling me an anecdote in a high voice accompanied by expansive gestures and saw a burly truck driver glowering at him, he sassed: "What are you looking at? I wouldn't kiss you for a dollar," and cowed the man completely.

In Sirmione the natives openly grinned at us as we passed on our evening stroll, for which Truman doused himself in Mitsouko, tied a Bronzini scarf around his neck and draped his jacket over his shoulders. But his getups were not necessarily the reason. One evening, parted from him for a few minutes, I returned to find him in the clutches of an aged and voluble Italian peasant who was gesticulating excitedly. Intervening with my smattering of Italian, I discovered that, through the custom in Italy of officially reversing first and last names, a confused rumor was circulating. The man, an ardent pro-American and Christian-Democrat, wanted to express his emotion and shake the hand of President Harry Truman's son.

After dinner, there were the Warrens. As academically agreeable as they were, the four of us formed an American colony. We played poker on a metal table in the hotel garden one night, went for a picnic supper on the beach beneath a full moon which rose like a disk of orange fire the next, on the third ate cornbread Cinina cooked as a treat and then took turns dancing with her to the music of the hotel's orchestra, which made every selection sound like the overture to *William Tell*. After two weeks, knowing how lonely I would be when I was eating by myself, and at the same time longing for the added concentration of that loneliness, I decided to start south, the opposite direction of the one Truman was headed, back to Paris and London before New York.

On his return to New York Truman wrote a highly romantic article about our departure from Venice and arrival in Sirmione, "To Europe."* The romanticism does not come, however, from his selectivity and shading of what he saw and experienced. It is much more audacious. He describes in Sirmione the rain-drenched flowers in a castle garden, a band of mysterious, harp-playing peasants, a trio of swans rustling the marble shore of the lake—whereas there was no castle with a garden, no harp-playing peasants, no swans in Sirmione or on its lake, whose water he describes as so ominously clear that he pictured gothic creatures moving in its depths and could never swim in it, even though we both swam in it every day. In his picture of Venice

*Collected in *Local Color*.

there is no strike, no soldiers, no violence; there is instead a "gruesome" persecution by a "wretched-smelling," sixteen-year-old Italian girl, the head of a band of cigarette-selling juvenile gangsters, making forays day and night into "our" rooms in those impenetrable-to-any-but-the-registered-paying-guests Venetian hotels, smoking pack after pack of cigarettes, drinking bottle after bottle of Strega, and finally, out of love for me, throwing at us a dead yellow cat wrapped in a newspaper and with a dollar watch tied around its neck—a recognizable refugee from Truman's fiction, but unrelated, like his description of Sirmione, to those "things whose strong reality outshines our fairyland" that had surrounded him in Italy.*

I finished *The Dog Star* in Florence and went on to Rome, to stay through the end of October. Meanwhile, in New York the only social gatherings to which Truman and I might both have been invited took place and were reported to me in letters by Truman and also by Sandy, who wrote that the television "News of the Day" on August 12 showed Truman and Tennessee—and only Truman and Tennessee, although Clark Gable, Spencer Tracy and Charles Boyer were among the passengers—disembarking from their crossing on the *Queen Mary*.

That fall was also probably the only time when Truman and Gore repeatedly encountered each other, during parties and gatherings at Tennessee's. Jo Healy, whom both Tennessee and I had known almost as long as we had been in New York, was there with her flash camera, like a prototype paparazzo, taking pictures left and right; she sent me one of Truman, Gore and Tennessee; and Sandy's letters carried forward the line of his letters from England and described Gore as in a continual fervor of attacking Truman. Truman, for his part, was enjoying himself. His letters to me never mentioned Gore.

Shortly after his arrival that August, Truman was detained by the police for illegally entering Buffie Johnson's two-story house on East Fifty-eighth Street, where Tennessee was staying. He was seen by two officers when, tired of waiting for Tennessee, late as usual for an appointment, he got in by climbing through a

*From Lord Byron's description of Venice, "Childe Harold," Fourth Canto, VI.

ground-floor window. While he and the police were there, Tennessee arrived with Gore.* But even in his letter about this evening, Truman fails to mention Gore; it is the incident's being reported in the gossip columns of Walter Winchell that delights him, together with his having bought a $400 suit at Knize to celebrate his having won "300 bucks" for the O. Henry Memorial short-story award.

One category of Truman's inventions I never thought of believing was the stories of how he seduced all the other boys in grammar school, before he was ten, and went to bed with all the other boys in high school. The first seemed to me halfhearted mythmaking, and although I have known a number of people who did or claimed to have done the second, there was very little reason to believe Truman's assertions in this case because he showed no inclination for promiscuous sex when I met him. I accepted these stories as the counterpart of the ones he told in those days, although they dropped from his repertory later, of how his divorced parents vied for his affection when he was not yet in his teens, and living with relatives in rural Alabama, by giving him competitive presents of Jaguar sports cars, Harley-Davidson motorcycles, etc. The believable note he struck with me in Sirmione, as he had earlier with Sandy in Paris, was that he wanted to be in love with and be faithful to someone who was in love with and faithful to him, but that he wasn't attractive enough and knew it: not a complaining note but a thoughtful one, embroidered with entertaining tales of his love life gone wrong. He clearly wanted to be loved, but friendship without sex seemed far more important to him than sex without friendship, although there was no reason to doubt that the combination was what he would have preferred.

That this was true was proved by a series of excited telephone calls he made to me soon after my return to New York in November. He had taken an apartment on Second Avenue between Fifty-eighth and Fifty-ninth Street (just around the corner from Buffie's house, where Tennessee was staying) and the pur-

*In his *Memoirs* Tennessee has metamorphosed this into "Truman and Gore, still on friendly terms at this point, had got a bit drunk together and had climbed in through the [front door] transom of the apartment to wait for me. . . ."

ported purpose of the calls was to let me know that he couldn't be reached there—he was in bed with a new friend in a cold-water flat on the Upper East Side and wasn't about to leave. Still in bed, haven't been up except to eat, was the message on the second day. And the third, with the teasing explanation that he could only talk for a minute, he was calling while his friend was out buying food. Or, to be more accurate, the truth was proved by the sequel to these calls, for this was the beginning of his friendship with Jack Dunphy—a former ballet dancer, formerly married to a ballet dancer—which was to continue for decades and had progressed far enough by March for the two of them to set off to Europe and to settle for the summer in Ischia, the first of the many places he and Jack, also a novelist, lived and worked in together during the coming years.

Tennessee, asked on his arrival from Europe if he had seen Truman in Paris before they sailed, replied: "Seen him! He was everywhere I looked." After my return to New York, I found that Truman's presence in the publishing world was as ubiquitous as Connolly had said his name was. My agent at the time was Audrey Wood. Early in March I asked her not to submit *The Dog Star* to Random House, where Truman suggested I should go on his recommendation; I didn't want to be involved with him businesswise and I thought it would be easy to keep from him what Audrey was doing. Not at all. The next thing I knew he was on the telephone; Random House was furious that I had submitted my novel to Knopf instead of to them. He knew, because Random House had called him and said Knopf had called them and asked if they had rejected my novel. The result, depressingly, was that both publishers turned the book down.

A few months later I took my novel away from Audrey Wood. I felt uneasy having it handled by someone who was representing both my and Tennessee's increasingly conflicting interests in the business of selling the film rights of *You Touched Me*. On my own I submitted the novel to Doubleday. The last day of September an editor there, Donald Elder, telephoned to say that they would like to publish it; he was off to Paris that afternoon; I should come in the following week to discuss a contract with another editor. Truman, with Jack, was still in

Europe, and I was eager to let him know that I had at last found a publisher. But not even this was possible. A note arrived the next week from Truman in Paris: Bravo! have just learned the wonderful news from Don Elder.

To me, Truman's letters from Ischia the spring and summer of 1949 are more interesting than his later article about the island. I've never been to Ischia, but the article reads as romantic as the one on Sirmione. Picturing his isolation, he says that at the post office he sees "the other Americans living here: there are four." His letters, on the other hand, call Forio a Mediterranean version of Fire Island and are chock-full of "almonds" of gossip, news—and this includes only the people in Forio whom I knew—of Tennessee and his lover, Frank Merlo, Bill Aalto and Jimmy Schuyler, Auden and Chester Kallman, and half a dozen others. The feuds between Auden's crowd, "the Santa Lucia set," and Truman's crowd, "the Di Lustro set," are recounted with gusto; and about Aalto and Schuyler, both of whom I was fond of, he wrote with feeling. Aalto had broken a grappa bottle over Schuyler's head and fled to Rome. Jimmy, with an opinion I later came to share, decided Aalto was insane and he wanted no more to do with him; but Truman, learning that Aalto sent Jimmy three letters a day, wrote me that although that might be a sign of insanity he, as a helpless romantic, thought it very sweet, for all the letters said was I love you, come back! come back!

Between Ischia and Paris, Truman visited North Africa. A letter from Tangiers contains his first mention of Gore, whom he ran into as soon as he was off the boat. He is now onto the game, but his only comment is: Oye! Incidentally, in this letter *he* tells *me* he has run into Cyril Connolly and that Connolly is going to publish a new story of mine in *Horizon*.

· 2 ·

By now it must be apparent to the reader that I am not including any of Capote's letters. Several years ago, our friendship ended; and since the right he had given me to publish his letters had been given in friendship, I returned it to him. The original purpose of this memoir is removed. Why have I taken it up again? How will I give my "nougat" flavor and texture without his "almonds"? First, there remains the information from Capote's letters; then there are the "almonds" in my journals, Sandy's and my letters, etc. But what I make will, in any case, be a different confection. As the italicized paragraph at the head of the first page of this new version indicates, it will go farther in time and story than I initially foresaw. The fact that the friendship has ended has now become the strongest reason to record it and the other lost friendships it touched. I am taking this up again out of a need to counterbalance a loss with understanding; and despite the unordinariness of the friends I am writing about, that is an ordinary need. Even though the situations I describe may be special in their details, the emotions and problems those situations led to are the familiar ones most people have to face sooner or later, trying to understand the reality around them when it doesn't resemble the reality they have been led to expect, trying to face, finally, that their own lives are going to end, even though they cannot comprehend it.

For, alas, friendship, like life itself, is limited. It has a mortality. "Early friends drop out," Graham Greene wrote, "like milk teeth." Late ones, too. All the same, as with life's, friendship's demise doesn't cancel its value. It doesn't negate its reality. And—although this puts me in opposition to Capote—it is reality I care about. Stories about real people being in places where they weren't, doing and saying things they never did or said, affront my sense of value. The invention that is difficult and essential in fiction strikes me as too easy here. Once, when I corrected Truman for saying that I had met Fred Melton in the barrel factory where I worked in Georgia, which was untrue, he replied: "Yes, but it's better that you should have met him in the barrel factory and I remember things the way they should have been." For that reason, it is doubtful that Truman will like much of what I have to say. I believe he now means it seriously when he quips lightly: "I don't care what anybody says about me as long as it isn't true." And it is likely that other people may accuse me of speaking ill of him. I have to take my cue from André Gide's journals, where he writes: "There is not one of my friends of whom, if I drew his portrait, I should not seem to be 'saying ill.' Love can be blind; friendship cannot; it owes it to itself not to be."*

At the end of March 1950, a month before *The Dog Star* was published, I set out alone for Europe, sailing on the *de Grasse*. Sandy was working with the Lunts in *I Know My Love* and wouldn't be free until June. Truman had returned to New York the previous December. (Hoping to help me get some publicity for my book, he took me in February to a party that was supposed to be photographed by *Life,* but *Life* didn't turn up.) He and Jack planned to go back to Europe, sailing soon after I did, on a Norwegian freighter. We agreed to meet in Naples, where they would land, and go together to Taormina.

Despite my small advance on the novel and one hundred dollars from selling the story to *Horizon,* I sailed with only a little more money than in 1948. Until the last moment, I was imprudently planning to leave with even less. Then, a few days before my departure, Montgomery Clift, with whom I had remained friends since *You Touched Me* closed at the beginning of 1946 and saw frequently whenever he was in New York, came by the apartment and gave me $750. He said he could take it off his income tax and that I could consider it a loan if things worked out as we were hoping they would. He had been trying since the summer before to buy the film rights to *You Touched Me,* as a prelude to his offering a package deal of himself and the

*André Gide, *Journals,* July 22, 1928.

play to Hollywood producers, and had been unable to get any response from Audrey Wood beyond her objection that Tennessee was already in too high a tax bracket to need any more income. But now Audrey had agreed to talk with Clift's agent and lawyer, contracts were being discussed, and he told me at a farewell dinner with Sandy, at Angelo's on Mulberry Street the night before I sailed, that he was optimistic. And so, instead of sailing with $250 I sailed with $500 and left $500 in New York to draw on.

Nevertheless, as before, the end of my money remained in sight. It was Holy Year and when I arrived in Rome a room that had cost 500 lire two years before was now 1,500 lire. Consequently, I didn't stay long. I was in Naples, waiting, on April 22, when Truman was to arrive. No one at the Excelsior, where he had said he would stay, admitted knowing of a reservation for him. No one, anywhere, could understand the name of the ship he had said he would arrive on. So the next day, still alone, I left for Taormina.

Taormina, in late April, smells as though it is enfolded in the center of a great sun-warmed flower. I checked into the Albergo Timeo and went for a walk. In the main square, a promontory high over the sea, a group of men and boys were tossing coins. As I passed, André Gide came out of the crowd. Eighty years old, he wore a battered felt shepherd's hat, pulled straight down all around, and a cloak which looked as though it were made out of an old horse blanket. A man in his late forties, seasonably dressed in blue linen and espadrilles, was with him. They crossed the square to a large American limousine, got in, and were driven away by a chauffeur. Back at the hotel I wrote a note, reminding Gide of our meeting two years before, mentioning that I had recently sent my novel to him in Paris, and asking if I could see him. Then I went and inquired if the *portier* knew where Gide was staying. Of course; he was staying in the hotel.

That evening in the dining room, midway of the meal, Gide came across to my table, asked if I was Donald Windham and took his copy of *The Dog Star* from beneath his arm. Pulling up a chair, he sat down and said that my book was the only thing he had brought with him to read on his vacation—a pleasing if not veracious bit of French flattery—and that although he had only arrived the day before and had just started it, he found the opening wonderful. After dinner, as I was leaving, he stopped me and introduced me to the man with him, Pierre Herbart. He hoped, he added, that they would see me the next day.

This was the beginning of a brief, but far-reaching, friendship. Gide's English was formal; my French impossible; Herbart, however, spoke English fluently, although he professed to be unable to read it. Our intimacy took a great step forward the next day when Gide and Herbart invited me to ride to the beach with them in the afternoon. I had to decline. I had made an appointment to see the one person I had an introduction to in Taormina, an Englishman, Bobby Pratt Barlow. When Gide heard his name, he threw his hands up in mock horror. He had known Pratt Barlow in North Africa during the war and had run into him face to face the day before in the Greek theater. Gide had pretended not to recognize him; Pratt Barlow was the world's greatest bore; and I would be very sorry if I kept my appointment.

Nevertheless, I kept it. That evening, as soon as we encountered, Gide and Herbart wanted to know my impression. I had liked Pratt Barlow and said so; also, that the only servant who appeared all the time I was at his house was a boy of twelve or thirteen with the blond hair and perfect face of a Botticelli angel, who brought us vermouth, took away the glasses, opened and closed doors, etc. The minute Gide heard this he began to arrange a visit with as much enthusiasm as he had celebrated his escape the day before. We were in the lobby. The *portiere* was asked to ring up Pratt Barlow; Gide got on the phone and said he had not recognized him in the Greek theater; his memory was fallible; but I had mentioned his name and my visit and he would like to call and pay his respects.

We went the next morning. Gide was delighted with little Beppe, who was as omnipresent as the day before, patting him on the head, complimenting his appearance, admiring his portrait by Oliver Messel, etc. Then Beppe disappeared and Gide, restless, was ready to go. When we were in the hallway, taking our leave, our host pointed out on his bookshelves a set of

Gide's *Journals* in the Knopf edition of the English translation. Gide had given Sandy an inscribed copy of the second volume in Paris two years before, saying that Knopf had sent him so many copies he didn't know what to do with them; but now Gide examined the books one by one, lost in his pleasure at discovering them there, excusing his absorption by saying that he had never seen the American edition before, and completely unaware of Beppe, who was passing back and forth a foot from him, carrying Pratt Barlow's lunch to a room at the end of the hall.

Every day, in our increased intimacy, Herbart shared with me a new incident of Gide's behavior. I record some of them, and the events here, not to add anything to the knowledge of Gide's character—his journals and his friends' writings about him are far more explicit on the subjects of his *tentatives amoreuses* and his *mélange d'avarice et de générosité*—but for the degree to which they throw light on that intimacy and to which that intimacy overlaps with my other stories.

The day after our visit to Pratt Barlow, Herbart accompanied Gide to the Taormina barber's, where a small boy lathered your face before a man shaved you. When the boy had finished lathering Gide, he said: "No, you haven't done enough for me," and made the boy continue lathering for nearly twenty minutes before he would let the man shave him. Another day, I ran into Herbart outside the hotel, convulsed with laughter. The evening before, Gide had picked up a small, black-haired Taormina boy in his teens but looking half his age. Gide possessed a key to a side door of the hotel, to save him the effort of having to walk the long way to the lobby to go in and out, and had taken the boy to his room. When he left, Gide gave him 200 lire, despite the boy's protest that it was too little. Later, Gide told this to Herbart, who replied that certainly it was too little, then went out, found the boy, bought him an ice cream and gave him 500 lire. But Herbart's reprimand bothered Gide all night. In the morning he decided to correct his behavior and after breakfast, putting 500 lire into a package of cigarettes, went out to the piazza and, as he told Herbart, gave it to "the little blond boy of last night." "Blond?" Herbart protested. "He had coal-black hair." "No." Gide shook his head. "The boy I gave the cigarettes to was a blond." Just before I encountered Herbart, he had taken Gide to the Corso, found the black-haired boy and made Gide give him 300 lire, not telling him that he had already given the boy 500 lire himself. None of us discovered who the blond was or what he thought of his present.

My conversations with Gide were more formal: what was the combination of flowers that produced the continual perfume of the air; what was the purpose of the small holes in the wall at the end of the hotel piazza, where we often sat and talked, in which the swallows built their nests; why was my English, written and spoken, easier for him to understand than that of other Americans? He had, after carrying *The Dog Star* under his arm every day for a week, finally finished it and was as complimentary as at the beginning. Elder, at Doubleday, learning that Gide was reading my book, urged me to ask him for a quote. I inquired of Herbart if this would be a good idea. He doubted that it would succeed. Gide had been so chagrined by the ridicule he had received from English and American readers because of his praise of John Steinbeck's work* that he had determined never again to comment on contemporary American writing. For my part, I didn't want to pursue the idea. Doubleday had disappointed me by putting a fulsome quote from Tennessee on the book jacket instead of the one from E. M. Forster I had asked them to use; and since publication they had refused to take an ad to quote Thomas Mann, who had singled out my book for praise among American novels in a press conference on his seventy-fifth birthday, reported in the *N. Y. Herald Tribune*. I didn't approach Gide—but, remembering Herbart's remark, I smiled when, a few years later, Steinbeck received the Nobel Prize, and I thought how tickled Gide would have been if he had lived to know it. He was so quick with *joie de vivre* at every happy moment. When I mentioned that *Strait Is the Gate* was one of my favorite novels, he stood up, put his arms over his head and, smiling, shook hands with himself like a victorious prize fighter.

And today, remembering Gide as I think ahead to the di-

* He had said in a wartime "Imaginary Interview" that reading Steinbeck gave him keener satisfaction than reading Faulkner or Hemingway and that some of Steinbeck's stories equal or surpass the best tales of Chekhov.

verse stories I have to tell now, I think back with many unan-swered questions in my mind, to these stories' contrasts to the story of this European writer who at eighty, within a year of his death, and having undergone his full share of physical and spir-itual difficulties, and a greater share than that of any of my friends of artistic and worldly success, was still turning out work as excellent as any he had ever done, was still full of the joy of life and of interest in others, and who, despite his abundant endowment of the egotism necessary to such a career, was mod-est enough in his journals to refer to *Strait Is the Gate* as "a nougat in which the almonds are good." And I remember that this man who passionately loved truth died in serenity and sur-rounded by his oldest friends.

Almost two weeks after my arrival in Taormina, on the morning of May 3, I was sitting at the café in the main square, reading my mail, when I heard Truman's familiar voice shrieking to me from across the piazza. He had just arrived and checked in at the "other" hotel, on the opposite side of the Corso from the Timeo. He and Jack, who was arriving that afternoon on a later train on which he could bring their Kerry blue terrier, Kelly, had been at sea twenty-one days. Truman ate lunch with me at the Timeo. That evening, both he and Jack (and Kelly: more later about Kelly and the importance of animals in Truman's and Jack's life together) had dinner with me. In be-tween, we started the search for a house for them. The vagueness of everyone we spoke to was unpromising; but the next afternoon, following a lead given us by the proprietor of a jewelry store on the Corso, we walked out the Messina gate to see Fontana Vecchia, the house D. H. Lawrence had lived in during the early 1920s, and they decided to rent it.

On our return, Truman accompanied me to the Timeo. In the hotel square, we came upon Gide, sitting on the low wall where he liked to take the sun. As neither he nor Truman greeted the other, I introduced them; and leaving aside Gide's unrecognizing acknowledgment, I realized from Truman's de-meanor, his sudden quietness, his failure to make any claim of friendship or acquaintance, that they 'had never met before. What I had taken to be one of Vidal's jealous libels was true.

Earlier, Herbart had told me that Albert Camus was staying that spring in his, Herbart's, house in the south of France. They were old friends. Now, when I asked Herbart what he thought of Truman's story of having been to bed with Camus, he labeled it as categorically impossible. Camus disliked effeminacy and in his opinion anything beyond Camus's having met Truman casually was unlikely. Herbart himself looked upon Truman with little sympathy, and the two of them never spoke. Several days later Herbart and Gide moved to a hotel on the beach at Mazzarró. Toward the middle of May, Herbart returned to France. Gide's daughter, Catherine, and her husband, Jean Lambert, came to stay with her father. Herbart was married at that time to Elisabeth Van Rysselberghe, Catherine's mother, and he asked his wife to read *The Dog Star* to him. This led Elisabeth Van Rysselberghe, who had just finished translating *Arden of Faversham* with Gide, to translate *The Dog Star*. With Gide's, Herbart's and Camus's help she arranged its publication by Gallimard, which had turned it down when Doubleday submitted it to them. Later that year, the last of his life, Gide, as she wrote me, went over the translation with her, helping her polish it.*

Pratt Barlow had two houses, the one in town where I had visited him with Gide, and another in the country. On one of their first days in Taormina, Truman, Jack and I, with Kelly, walked to see him at the country house. The journey was straight up the mountain, a hike of more than an hour, through a wild trail that made the primitive road to Fontana Vecchia seem a highway. Part of the time we wandered lost in a wheat field, terraced up the side of a steep incline, interspersed with splatters of daisies, poppies, and other "weeds," red, white, yellow and purple, and looking down on ever more distant vistas of the blue-green sea. Pratt Barlow, then about sixty, lived in this retreat during the week alone (except for servants) and in

---

*Later, both before and after her divorce from Pierre Herbart, I visited Elisabeth Van Rysselberghe at her house in Cabris. In the 1960's, when my autobiography, *Emblems of Conduct,* was published, she translated it, too, and arranged its acceptance by Gallimard.

At the time of Gide's death in 1951 she wrote me: "Dear Windham, I thank you for us all. What you may have heard is true: his death was admirable, worthy of his life, peaceful and conscious. He had said all he meant to say and deemed it unnecessary to live any longer. Fate was kind to him. But he leaves a sensible void to those who lived near him. I shall write later. *Bien amicalement*, Elisabeth Herbart."

town on the weekends, walking back and forth.* The house, serene and elegant, was full of Oriental art, Italian cupids, English books. By the time we reached it, I had learned something about Jack. He was, as was his way, difficult on the first part of the walk, while everything was going well. Then, when we got lost, and after we reached the house and there was trouble between Kelly and Pratt Barlow's dogs, and with Pratt Barlow himself, who was used to ordering everyone about, as recluses with servants are apt to do, Jack became the opposite of difficult; he became angelic; and I realized that he wasn't as complicated as I had thought. He simply didn't believe it when life was too pleasant; he was tense and difficult unless there was some difficulty. Then, life being as he expected it to be, he relaxed and became all agreeableness, the smoother of the waters.

Soon after Truman and Jack moved into Fontana Vecchia, they invited me to stay in one of the rooms. There was plenty of space; they were renting two floors of the three-story building, above the bottom floor inhabited by the owner. I declined; such closeness wouldn't work. However, I didn't want to stay on at the Timeo. It was remarkably cheap, like everything else in Sicily that year, but it cost more than I could continue spending. Clift had written me, forecasting what eventually happened, that clauses were being insisted on in the *You Touched Me* contract which he feared would make the selling of his package deal to a studio impossible. Discounting the unlikely arrival of royalties from my book, I would have to get along on the money I had. Happily, an antique-dealer acquaintance of Truman's arranged for me to rent a furnished apartment in the former Albergo Belvedere. The building was vacant, as it had been since the war, uninhabited except for the rooms on the ground floor occupied by the owners. For a pittance I was rented a large room on the top floor with a bath and an enormous terrace overlooking the whole range of the Cyclopean shoreline as far as Etna.

During my two months in that aerie, my expenses were

*Pratt Barlow had lived in Taormina the three years the Lawrences were at Fontana Vecchia. They had no servants; Frieda did the cooking, Lawrence the housecleaning, scrubbing the floors and the terrace, always stark naked. He was delighted to shock the natives, Pratt Barlow told me, and never realized that it was the sight of a man doing woman's work, not the sight of him "in puris naturalibus," that shocked them.

about one half what they had been at the Timeo. This was thanks partly to Truman's and Jack's second invitation—to join them for martinis and dinner every night. My lunch, which they sometimes shared if they were in town, consisted of the local bread and wine, cheeses and fruits, prosciutto or salami, which cost next to nothing. Each evening, while it was still light, I walked to Fontana Vecchia, up a path used only by peasants with goats and donkeys—more like a rock-strewn torrent bed than a country lane, with sudden boulders and drops, sometimes of a foot or more—and each night, after dark, I returned, rolling rather than walking back down to Taormina, so relaxed by food and drink that I suffered no more than a skinned knee or two.

Not only did I see Truman and Jack every evening and sometimes at the beach, I continued to see Gide and his daughter and son-in-law. They occasionally gave me a lift back from Mazzarró when they were going to Taormina, and they asked me to join them on trips to nearby towns. In Forza d'Agrò, I remember, Gide sat quietly, reading his Virgil, while Catherine, her husband and I, accompanied by the village urchins, made a fruitless search for the possessor of the key to the church we had come to see. But on the way back down the mountain Gide's attention was once more riveted on the outside world. Several times he asked Gilbert, the chauffeur, to stop the De Soto so he could get out to examine the wild flowers blooming in the crevices of the rocks at the roadside, and once he returned with caper buds and blossoms to dissect on the ride back.

Early in June, the morning of Trinity Sunday, Gide, accompanied by Catherine and her husband, left Taormina—Gide never to return. Up until then, neither he nor his daughter ever spoke to me of encountering Truman, although Catherine, like Herbart, enjoyed speaking English and telling me what her father was up to, mainly working on his dramatization of *Les Caves du Vatican*. Her husband, Jean Lambert, in his book *Gide Familier,* specifies what Truman was to them: a part of the street scene they were diverted by when they drove to Taormina to go to the bookstore and sit at the café in the central piazza. *"Nous regardions passer la faune étrangère et locale; de la première, un*

*spécimen particulièrement marquant, en dépit de ses proportions ré-
duites, nous était offert par Truman Capote."* That is all. Truman,
for his part, did not pretend to have any other face-to-face meetings with Gide. Once or twice, chattering away as he did every
night about the minutest events of the day, he mentioned seeing
him in the distance, but mainly he asked me for news of "the
old buzzard," as he called him.

Therefore, despite my knowledge of Truman, I was surprised
by the double audacity with which at the end of the decade in
his text to Richard Avedon's book of photographs *Observations*
he wrote a visually vivid and psychologically entertaining description of a supposed last meeting of their lives between André
Gide and Jean Cocteau, a meeting at which Truman himself was
present, in Taormina in the spring of 1950. No biographer of
Gide, as far as I know, has paid any attention to this description
of an event that never happened. First and foremost because
neither Gide nor Cocteau, both assiduous recorders of their
every encounter, has recorded any such meeting. Also because
both Herbart and Lambert, each a friend of Cocteau's as well as
of Gide's, have written of Gide's Taormina sojourn without noting this fabulous event, which would have been so notable. Nor,
as far as I know, has any French biographer of Cocteau picked
up this story, not only because Cocteau was not in Sicily in
1950, but also because Cocteau recorded, shortly after Gide's
death, a description of their last face-to-face encounter at Cocteau's house in Milly, Seine-et-Oise, in February, 1949. * Nevertheless, at least one American biographer of Cocteau has
repeated Truman's story as "the gospel truth," and virtually
every account of Capote's life and work includes it as a biographical fact.

Another decade later, Truman wrote in the introduction to
The Dogs Bark, his collection of "non-fiction" articles ("Everything herein is factual"), a simple and convincing account of an
equally imaginary conversation he had with Gide, the two of
them "seated together on a sea wall" in Taormina. During this
talk a remark by Gide is supposed to have suggested to Truman
the title for his book. In this introduction, despite his usual

* *France-Amérique,* March 4, 1951.

boldness, Truman hedges about the date of this encounter. He says he doesn't remember if it took place in late February 1950 (when neither Gide nor Capote was in Taormina) or in late February 1951 (when Gide was dead); but he is specific about the subject of their conversation. Gide is advising him to be less sensitive to criticisms of his work, advice Truman must often have given himself as he attributes it in other places to both Albert Camus and Willa Cather. This exchange and Truman's friendship with Gide have also become regular elements in studies of Capote. Now, on the paperback reprint of *The Dogs Bark,* which I have just bought, the Arab proverb Gide supposedly cited is put in quotation marks and followed by Gide's name as though he made it about the book itself.*

In the light of Truman's fictitious account of Cocteau in Taormina, I don't know if he ever knew Cocteau in Paris or some other place. I do know that for a number of years I saw in George Platt Lynes's apartment a needlepoint pillow, depicting an acanthus-leaf face, that Lynes's friend Jensen Yow designed and Lynes executed, working into the colors the pubic hairs of several of his lovers. After Lynes's death in 1955, it was among his possessions that were auctioned. Sometime later, it turned up in Truman's apartment. Knowing it unlikely that Truman had gone to the auction, I asked where he had gotten it. "Jean Cocteau designed and made it for me," he replied and added: "As a birthday present." Frequently since, I (as well as Jensen) have seen it in photographs of Truman's living room, reproduced in magazines, attributed to Jean Cocteau.

But in 1950 all of this was still in the future, and even farther in the future was the time when I would be upset by such inventions and when their universal acceptance would begin to have a deleterious effect on Truman.

The middle of June, Sandy arrived in Taormina. At the end

---

*Truman did not send me a copy of *The Dogs Bark* when it came out in 1973, as he had of all his earlier books. But I read the preface. Sometime later, I noted in my journal: "October 2, 1975. Find in the Virginia Woolf biography (1972) where Truman surely got his *The Dogs Bark* title he attributes to an old Arab proverb and Gide. 'That's why your encouragement is a draught of champagne in the desert and the caravan bells ring and the dogs bark and I mount—or shall in a few months—my next camel.' (*Virginia Woolf,* Quentin Bell, Vol. ii, p. 171)" of the month, he and I left to make a *giro* of Sicily and go north to Florence, where we had my story "The Hitchhiker" printed by the Tipografia Giuntina. Sometime that fall, Truman temporarily put aside *The Grass Harp,* on which he was working, and—most likely under the salutary influence of Jack's continual "For God's sake, Truman, why do you have to lie all the time?"—wrote an article on Taormina as sentient and evocative as his article on Venice and Sirmione was otherwise, and more nearly truthful than his later pieces were to be.

For me to read "Fontana Vecchia" today is to experience again the quiet pleasures of Taormina and its semideserted streets before the "economic miracle" turned it, like Sirmione, into a Hollywood movie set of tourist shops and hotels. The article echoes, sometimes, the gossip of Truman's letters that fall, his cook's troubles with her brother, the werewolf scare, Cecil Beaton's visit, and sometimes recalls remembered summer scenes, the wheat-harvest celebration at Fontana Vecchia where Truman danced with the peasant youths, the mile-long walk down paths and steps to the beach with its clear water, the not quite sane intensity of the midday heat over the countryside. And in this setting it presents, in perspective, a glimpse of Gide as Truman glimpsed him that spring in Taormina, an old man sitting on a stone wall in a small piazza, just inside the Messina gate.

$\cdot$ 3 $\cdot$

One subject in Truman's letters from Taormina that fall of 1950, not mentioned in "Fontana Vecchia" or elsewhere, was his reaction to "A Writer's Quest for a Parnassus," the travel article Tennessee wrote for the *N. Y. Times Magazine* toward the end of the summer. I bring it up here for the relation it has to certain things I want to recount later.

Tennessee's article contained the denouement to a series of events that started a year earlier. At that time I held back from Doubleday the first quote Tennessee sent for the book jacket of *The Dog Star;* it said that my book introduced the finest young talent to appear since Carson McCullers. This wording made me think, for a number of reasons, that Tennessee was using the occasion to put down Truman and also Gore. He was feeling rivalry toward both of them at the time and had recently gone out of his way to snipe at them, in his review for the *N. Y. Times Book Review* of Paul Bowles's *The Sheltering Sky,* with disparaging remarks about "precociously knowing" young writers.

Somewhere Gide has attributed the lack of literary success of a friend to his failure to learn the art of making enemies. Perhaps I shared that failing in those days. In any case, in his travel article Tennessee paraphrased the statement I had held back. He wrote: "I have not yet been to Sicily this year. Truman Capote has unfurled his Bronzini scarf above the fashionable resort of Taormina. He is supposedly in D. H. Lawrence's old house. Also there, I am told, is André Gide and the young American writer Donald Windham, whose new novel *The Dog Star* contains the most sensitive new writing since Carson McCullers emerged ten years ago."

Truman's letter about the article reached me in Venice, where I was staying on the Giudecca in a sublet apartment where he and Jack joined me for a few days later on. After asking if anyone has sent me the article, he describes it in case no one has. Then he lets go in an outburst which convinced me that my instinct as to what he would feel about Tennessee's quote had been right. He denounces the vulgarity of Tennessee's writing throughout, including the paragraph about us, which he quotes to underline that although it contains a "plug" for my book it will do me no good in so low a context. And about Tennessee himself he spares no words.

This outburst is unique in Truman's correspondence with me, a sign of how sensitive he was to criticism of his work, even implied, and how hurt he was by the desire in a person he thought had become a friend to wound him in the area where he was most vulnerable.

· 4 ·

If such an outburst was unique in Truman's letters, it was nonexistent in encounters with him. As I have said, he liked people and wanted to be liked; he charmed. Throughout the 1950's it was a pleasure to share the enthusiasm with which he embraced his growing fame. A good deal of my contact with him during the decade was by letters, for he was largely in Europe and I stayed in the States. But he turned up on and off. He was back in New York briefly, once or twice, in 1951 and 1952, for the publication of the book, and the rehearsals and opening of the play, of *The Grass Harp*. On each occasion he enjoyed telling me how he needled Ken McCormick, the editor-in-chief of Doubleday, whenever they met at a party, for Doubleday's having turned down my second novel and dropped me as an author. Then one day early in January 1954, he telephoned unexpectedly. His mother had committed suicide; he had flown in from Paris the night before. Two afternoons later he came by the apartment and told us of the emotional and financial difficulties that had led to this. At the beginning he refused the martini he was offered, then he changed his mind and the three of us drank and talked until the gin bottle was empty.

I had first met Truman's mother in the apartment at 1060 Park Avenue, where she lived with his stepfather, Joe Capote, when Truman gave an after-theater party there during the winter of 1948-1949. It was a lively and crowded evening, the rooms full of writers and actors. Mr. Capote's Latin openness stood out in the gathering, magnified by his pride in the guests, but Nina Capote presided with the proper charm of a small, blond Southern woman. She and I came to know each other better during the fall of 1950 in Italy, when she and Truman's stepfather were in Venice on a holiday. Truman and Jack (and Kelly, his coat bleached a henna hue by the Mediterranean sun) came up from Sicily for a week. Every evening, cocktails at Harry's Bar were followed by dinner at an elegant hotel; and on September 18 Nina and Joe gave Truman a small cocktail party to celebrate the publication in New York of *Local Color*.

The apartment at 1060 Park Avenue, where Truman stayed when he did not have a place of his own, was depressing to visit that winter. The few times I was there the sun never reached the living room, in which I remembered having sat with Truman on the couch on bright afternoons a few years earlier and chattered cheerfully.* The dining room, facing it, looked dusty and dark, as though it had never been used. On my first visit, his step-father, with whose complicated financial troubles Truman had to deal, as well as with his mother's death, was seated at the table but quickly rose and disappeared. I met his aunt, his mother's sister, a small, pleasant Southern woman like her, who was there; and another day I met his father, Archulus Persons, a heavy man with a full face, whom Truman, slim and blond, like his mother, did not resemble then but was to look increasingly like in later years.

Facing tragedy, Truman displayed his characteristic boldness. Not very long after his return, he organized an evening for his friends to go to the Latin Quarter to see and meet Christine Jorgensen, who sang "When you walk through a storm, keep your chin up high." Then he immersed himself, day and night, in the production of the musical he had written from one of his short stories, "House of Flowers." I remember his reading the first act at the apartment of Saint Subber, the producer, one spring night, with Harold Arlen, the composer, playing the piano and singing the songs. Hedda Stern and Sol Steinberg, who was to design the sets—a project that fell through—were there, and Sandy and I. Later that summer the two of us joined Truman and Arlen several evenings, journeying from nightclub to nightclub, listening to singers they were considering for the cast. Early one morning, Arlen left the three of us at the Key Club, an after-hours bistro in an off-Fifth Avenue

*When he was breaking up the apartment, Joe Capote offered to sell Sandy and me the couch for a few dollars. He and his Cuban moving men brought it to our walk-up on Madison Avenue. They couldn't get it up the narrow staircase and had to take it away.

townhouse, where we sat until dawn, observing a speakeasy atmosphere I had never encountered before except in the pages of Fitzgerald and Van Vechten. At the next table, a drunk who looked like a stockbroker shouted every few minutes, "Play 'A Slow Boat to China,'" and held out handfuls of ten-dollar bills to the pianist. Just before we left, the drunk rose and staggered out, leaving his overstuffed chair upholstered in greenbacks.

Behind Truman's boldness, I was aware of what he was going through.

My journal: "August 9. Loneliness. One day last week, T. telephoned at ten A.M.; he was half asleep; it was as though *I* had telephoned and awakened *him*. 'I'll call you back,' he said; 'I just wanted to see if you were home.' And on Saturday the telephone rang in the afternoon. When I answered, there was no one there, just a droning, then a clattering, then T. picked up the receiver. 'I was across the room,' he said. 'I phoned earlier and you didn't answer so I thought you'd gone away for the weekend. I just called to check and I was doing something across the room, but then I heard the phone stop ringing. I'm going to Harold's to work now, but I'll call you later and we'll do something for supper.'"

What he put forward, however, was his self-deprecating sense of humor.

"September 8. Two nights ago we agreed to meet T. at a movie, then couldn't make it. Yesterday he said he spent the whole time looking for us in the loge and orchestra: 'I spent more time walking than if I'd been in a Turkish bath.'"

Nevertheless, he still worked at the mental prestidigitation he used in order to see himself as the person he wanted to be taken for.

"The other day, talking about *House of Flowers*, T. said: 'I do hope it's a success. Not for the money, but because it's the kind of show that I enjoy and would like to be able to go and see once a week if I wanted to. And even after a show opens, if it isn't a success, there are so many worries to distract you that you can never really relax enough to enjoy yourself.' He wasn't exactly trying to deceive himself, just sort of sneaking up on the idea."

Whatever my friendship meant to Truman that year, his meant a great deal to me. American book publishers were already entrenching themselves in the conviction that whatever my writing might be as art, it was not an article of commerce. I was unhappy, also, in a number of ways that have little to do with what I am telling here. I had finally learned—alas, not well enough!—that for anyone who was not a masochist or an opportunist it was wise to have as little as possible to do with Tennessee. This disillusion made it difficult for me to see a number of people we knew in common. As early as January, soon after Truman's return, a depressed entry in my journal lamented the lack of warmth I felt toward many old friends, the artificiality and impersonality that had grown up between us: "Except Sandy, only with Truman do I feel any easy relationship, any closeness in common."

We had few mutual concerns, true, but we were concerned with each other's concerns.

During the summer of 1956, Sandy and I spent a week with Truman in a house he and Jack had rented in Stonington, Connecticut. We were all working; Truman was dieting as well. His lunch was a tomato and cottage cheese, and he denied himself anything to drink before five o'clock, when a whistle blew in the shipyard across from the house. Then, having mixed a pitcher of martinis, he pantomimed a palsied drunk having his first drink of the day by tying his handkerchief around his right wrist, hooking the handkerchief around his neck and pulling it with his left hand to raise his right, which clutched his glass, to his lips.

One day he asked me into his bedroom—where he worked, usually stretched out on the bed—and gave me the manuscript of a half-completed novella to read. Truman's writing had not interested me before I knew him. Despite his verbal skill, his stories possessed no reality for me. I felt no admiration for them, such as I felt for Tennessee's. But after we had been together in Sirmione, I was interested in what he wrote. He read me finished stories there and in Taormina. I liked *The Grass Harp* more than *Other Voices, Other Rooms* and told him so. But, although by the 1950s we talked about writing—writing we had done, not writing we were going to do—it was not until this year, with "A Christmas Memory," a story as real as Chekhov's, that he won my unreserved admiration. When I finished reading the half-completed novella, he said that he wanted to title it *Breakfast at Tiffany's.* * This was my title for a book of stories I had been working on about sex between servicemen and civilians during the war. I had lost hope for my book and gladly gave the title to him. In any case, it originally had been given to me by Lincoln Kirstein when I was working for him.

That fall, Truman read the first draft of my novel about a playwright, *The Hero Continues.* Before starting my manuscript he warned me that he thought I should have written a *roman à clef* about Tennessee. (I had told him that I hadn't and didn't intend to.) After finishing it, he advised me still to do so, to capitalize on the scandals I knew about Tennessee, to change the male literary agent to a portrait of Audrey Wood, to portray Frankie Merlo, etc. A few years later, when he read the published version, which I had completely rewritten, but not in his direction, his comment was: "Oh, dear, it *is* a whitewash."

The next summer, visiting Truman, this time in Bridgehampton, both Sandy and I read the first draft of "The Duke in His Domain," the article on Marlon Brando he was writing for *The New Yorker.* Discussing Brando afterward, Sandy, who had worked with him for a year on Broadway, told of his first sight of Marlon sleeping on a table on the stage of the New Amsterdam Roof, where he had gone for a rehearsal of *A Streetcar Named Desire.* When the article appeared, Truman had incorporated this experience beautifully, transferring it to himself.

Truman's letters, also, dealt more at this time with our various concerns than with gossip. He expressed pleasure when we each had a story in the same issue of *Botteghe Oscure.* He asked questions and gave advice about my dealings with publishers. He hoped I'd gotten a Guggenheim. He bemoaned my hepatitis, his flu and his allergy to seafood. He sent facts about the local fish for a Sicilian story I was writing. He entered into my prob-

* Two autobiographical echoes in *Breakfast at Tiffany's* interested me: of Truman's recent visits to Joe Capote at Sing Sing, where his financial difficulties had landed him, in Holly's visits to Sally Tomato at Sing Sing; of Nina Capote's real given name, Lillie Mae, in Holly's Lulamae.

lems with the pet toad and newt I kept in a herbarium and had to feed live flies, and sent news of Jack, "insulting more people," and Kelly, "biting more dogs than ever," and eventually of "all five" of them, for to Kelly were added an English bull pup, Bunkie, and a Greek cat, Diotima. He asked me to undertake various commissions, to search for an apartment for him in New York, to look among our photographs for one of him he could use to apply for a visa, to send him several of the notebooks he wrote in. There was some gossip, too. He commented on the rumor that Tennessee and Diana Barrymore were to be married, asking if to her biography, *Too Much, Too Soon*, I thought she was planning a sequel, *Too Little, Too Late*. And when there was no news or he was bored, his letters slipped into primitive expressions of affection in the schoolgirl tone of his salutations, *Peaches Precious, Honeyheart,* and his closings, *Oodles of passion, Hugs, Miss you 25 hours a day*.

Still, he hated it when he had nothing interesting to say. A letter from Taormina, at what must have been a particularly dull moment in April 1951, mentions offhand that Eugene O'Neill has turned up there—a nervous little man at loose ends and lonely, but rather likable—an offhandedness that was transparently fictional—without my knowing that O'Neill was in Doctors Hospital in New York, unable to walk—as soon as I thought of the dramatic presentation such a reality would have brought.

When he was busy and full of news that he had no time to dramatize, an unguarded truth or two could slip out. In December 1952, from Rome where he was working on the script of *Terminal Station* for De Sica, he tells me that my friend Montgomery Clift is in the cast and, without disguising that he hasn't known him before, describes how much he likes him, despite Monty's rewriting of his dialogue. About the same time, in another letter he writes that it isn't safe to go out on the streets except heavily veiled because Carson McCullers, "Sister," and her husband, Reeves, "Mr. Sister," are in Rome and Truman and they don't speak.

But, fact or fiction, the letters were pleasant to receive. The exaggerations were harmless, as when on a later trip to Taormina Truman found Fontana Vecchia unavailable and wrote that he and Jack had rented an entire hotel, twenty-two rooms and six baths. That was his manner. Had mine been the same, I might have said something similar when I was the sole guest in the empty Albergo Belvedere.

In 1958, when he and Jack were staying on the Greek island of Paros, Truman's correspondence was almost entirely on postcards. One that I particularly liked, that I felt expressed the ease between us, depicted a bas-relief of a stooped Bacchus, bearing the weight of the world on his shoulders. It asked only: Why does this remind me of you?

By that time I was feeling the weight of my situation. After *Horizon* folded, I had published four stories in the BBC magazine *The Listener,* whose literary editor was J. R. Ackerley. But I was having no more success than usual in the States. Needing money, I had worked at Sherry's in 1952 delivering liquor, and at Bloomingdale's in 1953 opening packing cases. I wrote a play, *The Starless Air;* it was tried out in Houston, but my expenses there exceeded my royalties. Recommended by José Quintero, who was to direct, I worked on a dramatization of *The Baker's Wife;* the producers lost their shirts on another play and the production fell through. I adapted for the stage a novel by Isak Dinesen, *The Angelic Avengers.* Roger Stevens optioned it and sent me to Paris and Rome for two weeks to see Lars Schmidt, who was to be co-producer, and Baroness Blixen (Isak Dinesen: She put me at my ease the evening we met, saying, "Plays are sometimes better than the novels they are adapted from, *La Dame aux Camélias,* for example." We became friends and I will speak of her again.) The play was scheduled to open in England; then that production, too, fell through. I had completed two revisions of *The Hero Continues,* but not found a publisher. I was at a low point professionally and was financially insolvent.

Truman's situation was, as usual, very different from mine, but he was not without his problems. In one letter that congratulated me on having started a new novel, he expressed doubt that he himself would ever write another. He just seemed to keep tearing up pages, a process that would have to stop but to which he could foresee no end. I took this to mean he was feeling, not that he had exhausted or come to the end of his subject matter, so much as that his subject matter no longer satisfied or interested him. Perhaps that his subject matter was, after all, not so much his as it was other people's that he had coveted; that it was no longer a worthy object for the skill he had developed in writing; and that its value didn't repay the effort he expended on it. Early on, talking to me about other authors, he would say, "Well, we know we're good writers, don't we?" His ambition was to be a good writer, not to write well on a subject that was demanding to be written by him. His subjects were not the source of his drive; they did not demand all of it; and thus there was all that invention left over, after they were completed, to go into his making up biographical fantasies about his earning a living by painting imaginary flowers on glass, his being the protégé of a well-known fortune-teller, his ghostwriting speeches for a Southern politician, to go on his book jackets; and there was still enough drive left to overflow into his personality and fuel his selling of himself, at which he was a past master. He was beginning to feel the need of subject matter which was not secondhand, which he had chosen for a reason other than that he recognized it as "literary" from other writers' use of it, subject matter that had no importance except what his skill and ambition allowed him to pour into it. He was already feeling this when he decided to write *The Muses Are Heard;* but in that book and in the article on Brando he was trading in personalities, his own and other people's. The "known" qualities of these supplied so much advantage that there was still a surplus of the energy generated by his opposition to reality. The conventional amount of fiction he had worked into *The Muses Are Heard,* the conventional amount of factualness that, through the first-person narrator, he had carried over into *Breakfast at Tiffany's* (with its mélange of echoes) didn't satisfy him. He was beginning to feel not so much dissatisfied with his work as so aware of his power, technical and promotional, that his work did not seem up to it. Or am I lending him too much of my own feelings?

In any case, he was about to bid "goodbye" to, I won't say the kind of writing by which he had made his reputation, but the kind of writing he had been doing *while* he made his reputation.

He was ready to develop a manner of combining subject

matters to which—though it may be misleading in the extremity of its example—a key may be found in the mixture of invention and reality ("real toads in imaginary gardens" is his phrase in *Music for Chameleons**) that he used in his description of Gide's and Cocteau's "farewell encounter" in Taormina.

In 1959, important changes came about for both Truman and me. In my case, the changes were simple. I escaped the impasse I was in. Rupert Hart-Davis in England accepted *The Hero Continues*. Then he agreed to publish a collection of my short stories and E. M. Forster volunteered to write an introduction for it. *Noonday* in New York published my translation of Pierre Herbart's book on Gide, *A la recherche d'André Gide*. More important, financially and professionally, was another breakthrough, brought about by Truman. After reading one of my autobiographical pieces in *The Listener,* he wrote that I should submit the new ones to William Maxwell at *The New Yorker;* Maxwell would like them. I was dubious; I had been submitting my work to the magazine for years without success; but I took Truman's suggestion. It worked. By the end of the year, *The New Yorker* had accepted three stories, had offered me a first-reading agreement and was soon to buy four stories more.

In Truman's case, the changes were more complicated; but they centered in two events, one at the beginning, one toward the end of the year. Each was to have a marked, and a mixed, effect on his life and work. In January, he won me anew, and practically everyone else who saw him, by his appearance, together with Norman Mailer and Dorothy Parker, on David Susskind's TV talk show *Open End*. Then, in November, he read the news item about a multiple murder in Kansas which started him to work on *In Cold Blood*. But the decade ended, as it had begun, with Truman still the vulnerable person, aware of other people's feelings, he had been when I met him ten years earlier, still the charmer, enjoying his social give and take with the world, making a gift of himself, asking to be liked. A review of the Susskind program in *The New Republic* by Janet Winn (now Janet Malcolm) exactly caught his quality.

*I don't know if he intended this phrase to be taken as his or as a quote from Marianne Moore, whose words are "imaginary gardens with real toads in them" ("Poetry," in *Selected Poems*).

"Mr. Capote may *look* effete, but he is not: his mind is vigorous and extremely able. He speaks slowly, often stops to choose his words, and makes every word count. What he says invariably makes excellent sense. His sensibility also proved to be remarkable. He demolished Mr. Mailer's arguments at every turn, but he never 'scored.' He seemed always keenly aware, as few panelists ever are, that this was a social and public event, as well as a debate, and that accordingly he must see to it that Mr. Mailer not be made to feel uncomfortable . . ."

And this is a combination of traits not as common as one might think.

· 5 ·

"It is worse winning than losing."
—Jack Dempsey

The pleasure with which Truman enjoyed his success in the 1950s was accented by its contrast to the misery with which Monty and Tennessee suffered theirs.

I have recorded in the book of Tennessee's letters to me my liking for him, the pleasure it was for me to be with him in his salad days—from 1940 on. He was the one person I loved to whom I did not have a physical attachment. In the early years our concerns were mutual, or at least I felt that they were. His devotion to his work inspired me. Even after his success, our senses of humor, our passions, our aims as writers remained similar in my eyes. His inscriptions in the copies he gave me of his first three published plays, which I still have, suggest that he felt the same: *Battle of Angels,* TO DONNIE WHOM I MET FIRST IN N.Y. AND HOPE TO KNOW LAST, EVER; *The Glass Menagerie,* TO WINDHAM WHO FIRST APPROVED, WITH LOVE; *A Streetcar Named Desire,* TO A FELLOW PASSENGER, WITH LOVE.

For ten years I looked forward with excitement to his company. By the 1950s, however, encounters with him, although unlikely to be dull, were unlikely to be pleasant.

During this decade he began not only no longer to prefer his work to himself, as Gide says an artist must, but no longer to prefer his work to his box-office statements. As early as 1951, when Sandy was playing with the Lunts in Chicago, in a theater which shared a backstage alley with the one where *The Rose Tattoo* was giving its pre-Broadway engagement, he witnessed the beginning of this change. Each night when his scene was not on, he went across and stood with Tennessee and the director,

Daniel Mann, at the back of their theater. Tennessee was counting the laughs in each scene and, when there were not enough to make him feel "box-office" secure, suggesting the insertion of gags similar to those he had fought to prevent Eddie Dowling from putting into *The Glass Menagerie* six years earlier. The commercial failure of *Summer and Smoke,* after the successes of *Menagerie* and *Streetcar,* had unnerved him.

By 1955, commercial success was so important to him that he fled from the Broadway opening night of *Cat on a Hot Tin Roof,* appalled by the sabotage he had wreaked on his play in order to keep Elia Kazan, whom he had come to consider a touchstone of audience appeal, as director. He denounced the production as a betrayal of what he had intended and berated Kazan to the press. Then, looking at the box-office statements, he praised Kazan for having made his play a success and berated the press for having reported his earlier remarks. Before the end of the decade, he would repeat the same process with *Sweet Bird of Youth.* He could no longer keep going without the "fix" of a commercial hit, no matter what the price; and as the sixties approached, suspecting everyone of judging him as he judged himself, he was washing down Seconals with double martinis, looking toward psychoanalysis as a cure-all for his troubles—as he would look toward injections of speed in the next decade—and announcing with despair: "I am tired of living with myself as I am." Whenever he encountered old friends, he felt a compulsion to make them suffer as he was suffering; he was becoming an expert in deliberate cruelty.

Monty's difficulties were different from Tennessee's and Truman's. And my friendship with him was different from mine with them. I knew the two of them much better than I knew him; but my friendship with Monty had a physical side that did not exist in their cases. There was a mutual, or rather a general, physical attraction. When Monty came to the apartment we often went to bed, and more often than not he spent the night with us, all three sleeping sardine-packed on the bed's three-quarter-size mattress. There was mutual admiration, too; he was sympathetic to my attitude toward writing, and I was sympathetic to the extreme idealism of his attitude toward acting. He had a higher standard for himself in his work than anyone else I have known in his profession. Therefore, I found it hard to believe when, in 1953, I was told by an actor who was working with him in Hollywood that Monty had begun to turn up drunk on the set of *From Here to Eternity*. But I soon saw for myself that he was undergoing a radical change. He still called when he was in New York between films, and he never ceased to try to keep up our old rapport, but it became increasingly difficult. When we met, his mind, behind the affectionate phrases, would seem to be elsewhere. Even before his alcoholic behavior became chronic, a mental or spiritual suffering was shutting him off from people. After his automobile accident in 1956, in which his face was smashed up and his teeth knocked out, physical suffering was added. And to the alcohol were added pain-killing drugs.

I do not know what brought about Monty's disintegration. He did not have the burden Tennessee had—and I do not underestimate its difficulties—of having been catapulted overnight from obscurity to celebrity; he had been playing featured roles on Broadway for ten years. From the little I can understand, I believe the cause must have been a deep disillusionment. He won and then discovered that the game was not worth the effort, that the values were not those he had believed in. The prize was counterfeit. This would agree with the timing of his malaise, from the moment he became a "star" and a prized commercial commodity, and with his continual dissatisfaction with the scripts submitted to him and with what the directors he worked for wanted from him. He realized that the attraction his employers valued in him had little relation to the potentialities he valued.

I do not think his disintegration had anything to do with the conflicts of his sexual nature. One of his biographers makes this the theme of her biography, and I regret that I talked to her when she was researching her book—not that I told her much or anything intimate—as I have regretted it each time I have talked to any journalist about anyone I knew. (Among my reasons for taking up this memoir again, I failed to mention Truman's persistent pressures on me to talk to anyone who was writing about him, pressures *he* made me regret giving in to whenever I did. The first was for an article in *Esquire* by a journalist whose opening question was: "Do you agree with Gore

Vidal that Capote is a pathological liar?" When I refused to say more than that his reality is not mine, and thenceforth evaded the journalist's leading questions, so that this was my only observation he quoted, Truman said indignantly: "Well! you didn't have much of interest to say about me.")

I knew people Monty had been to bed with many years before me, and my belief was that he had adjusted in his teens to his sexual inclinations. (We were exactly the same age and still in our twenties when all this was going on.) His degree of secrecy about his lovers, as about his friends, seemed to me a kind of generous greediness, a desire to have more of each by keeping them all separate, and not shame or an inability to accept. That his behavior in regard to sex went to pieces when he disintegrated is neither here nor there; his behavior went to pieces in every respect. But the central collapse was the loss of his devotion to, almost his reverence for, his work, his pervading inability to adhere to the standards that had motivated him from the beginning, even though he strove to adhere to them until the end.

In my experience, Monty was never deliberately cruel; but after a certain point each encounter with him made anyone who was fond of him suffer.

My journal: "December 13, 1958. The telephone rings between noon and one o'clock. Sandy answers. It is Monty, calling to ask us to a sneak preview of his new film, *Miss Lonelyhearts*. I listen on the other phone. Really a voice from the grave. Long silences blurred by the slur of articulation trying to begin a word, like someone waking out of a drugged sleep and slipping off again between syllables. S. asks if he has talked to Bill. 'Wwwwhat d'you think's his problem? Being a Negro?' They are talking about different Bills. Monty asks about me. S. answers. A long pause. A blur of articulation. 'Start again.' Monty makes a rather complicated statement about Truman, as though his mind works subtly but blanks out in the effort of communication, despairs of reaching another person, yet is angered by the difficulty of something once so simple; and in answer to S.'s saying that he doesn't know what he means, says with only slightly faded force and continuity, 'You know damned well what I mean. Sometimes somebody presents an argument and the argument is no good but their charm convinces you.' Then statements so confused it is impossible to know if they are about Truman or me. Then silence. S. says for him to come and see the play he is in. Silence. S. says for him to take care of himself. Long silence. S. says, 'No answer to that?' Silence. 'Yes?' Silence. 'Yes?' After a while a voice, speaking so faintly it can only be to itself, sighs, 'Just keeps saying yes, yes, yes.' 'And maybe we'll see you sometime?' S. says. Longer silence than ever. There is still no reply when S. hangs up.

"Each time this happens, one has a terrible feeling of having failed someone in need. I am convinced that one could not escape failing him no matter what one did, even if one went right over to his house and tried to see him. I am ashamed, nevertheless, for I cannot believe that the call does not come from some need, and I know that one should try to respond despite a conviction that there is no possibility of success. It is like the moans of a dying man, on the pavement at the side of some shattered wreck, to which one listens helplessly. Helpless to go back ten years. Or to cover the same distance he has.

"Four hours later, between four and five, the telephone rings and this time I answer. It is Monty again. He begins, as he did with S., by asking if I want to go see his movie; but this time he sounds perfectly natural, waits while I get a pencil to write down the place and time, which, incidentally, is Monday night, although he asked Sandy for Wednesday. The whole conversation is coherent and like one long ago; and as I do not mention it, I don't know if he realizes that he called before. I wish I had brought it up. I would like to know."

The passages in my journals about Tennessee in those years are too depressing, their ramifications too far-reaching, for me to copy out any of them here. They need a place of their own. A brief summary of the pertinent points of one will suffice. For a time I hesitated between choosing the afternoon he cajoled William Inge, just back from a sanatorium for alcoholism, "Come on and celebrate with me, Bill; one little glass of champagne won't hurt you"; and the night he accompanied Carson McCullers on the stage of the Y.M.H.A., for her talk on her career as a writer, and increased her nervousness by pushing the microphone back and forth in front of her, read passages from her work other than those she asked for to illustrate her point, then leaned back, smoking his cigarette and smiling thoughtfully. But I think the following, which occurred several years before the conversation with Monty, is more typical.

Maria Britneva, a young actress, had arrived from England. As she and Sandy and I were friends since 1948, Tennessee telephoned a few days before Christmas and invited us to dinner with them on Christmas Eve. The next day he had Maria ring up and say they had decided it would be pleasantest to have dinner at our place. The occasion was, to say the least, nervous-making. After we had eaten, Tennessee called Maureen Stapleton to ask her for Marlon's telephone number so we could go to visit him. When Tennessee hung up, he said it sounded as though there were lots of people at Maureen's so why didn't we stop there first. We met an odd reception when we arrived. Maureen was in a state of maudlin depression; the gathering was a kind of wake by her friends to console her for having been turned down that day as a choice to repeat her leading role in a proposed London production of *The Rose Tattoo*. When one of the guests, another young actress, Maggie McNamara, angrily brought this up to Tennessee, he grinned sheepishly and said, "Oh, I don't think there's been any final decision on that." Shortly afterward, we left to see Marlon, who at that time had an apartment across the street from Maureen, in Carnegie Hall. We didn't get beyond the lobby there. Marlon exited from the elevator as we were about to enter, said he was on his way out, and after a few coolly polite words departed.

Yes, indeed, seeing Truman in those days, after encountering Monty or Tennessee, was like a breath of fresh air, and a much-needed help toward believing that it was, after all, *possible* for an artist to enjoy worldly success in America.

· 6 ·

From Spain, where he was holed up with Jack on the Costa Brava, Truman wrote a long letter in October 1960, about his progress, his worries, his plans for *In Cold Blood*. He had nearly finished the first of the four parts. To his dismay, it ran over 35,000 words. The whole book, he figured, would be over 125,000. A length problem was new to him and he did not know how the book could be cut. Still, he could see that *The New Yorker,* which was to serialize it, might not be willing to devote four full issues to so unpleasant, so "unentertaining," a subject, in which case he wouldn't be able to recover from that source the formidable sum he had invested in gathering his material. Whatever might happen, however, he was now committed to the book, despite the devastating effect his subject matter was having on him. It was leaving him increasingly limp, numb and horrified. The objectivity he had begun the book with was gone. He was involved emotionally with his characters, unable to get them out of his mind, and had awful dreams every night.

This was the first of many communications in the same vein over the next four years. I received it in Denmark. After my other good luck had made a grant unneeded, the Guggenheim Foundation, following ten years of applications, had given me one. As the brownstone where Sandy and I had lived since we met was being torn down, we stored our possessions in a friend's basement and went to Europe for a year, taking a Greek freighter to Piraeus. In Greece we stayed in many places, including the Villa Meltimi on Paros, which Truman's postcards had led me to assume was a villa he rented, but which was the island's small tourist hotel. Greece, however, did not turn out to be a place where I could work well. By early fall we had traveled north through Italy and Germany to Denmark and were living in a small, thatchroofed cottage which Clara Svendsen, Isak Dinesen's companion, had lent us.

Isak Dinesen was one of the first people I knew who felt hurt by Truman. She had written an introduction to the Danish translation of *Breakfast at Tiffany's*. The book had recently been published and Truman had asked me to send him a copy, as he hadn't received one. When I saw Baroness Blixen—she had a cluster of names besides her nom de plume, Isak Dinesen, and her legal name, Karen Blixen; her family pet name was Tanne and Clara habitually called her Tania—and told her that I had bought a copy of *Holly,* as the translation was titled, for Truman, she said that she had been so upset by the description he had written of her in *Observations* that she had considered withdrawing the introduction. All her friends advised her to do so. But, in the end, she decided that this would be unprofessional. She had written it and she suppressed her feelings and let it be printed.

Truman's description of having tea with Isak Dinesen at Rungstedlund is similar in verbal skill and carefully worked-in documentation to his trompe-l'oeil description of Gide and Cocteau in Taormina. However, there is no doubt that this event occurred, as there is no doubt that she charmed him and he charmed her. His presentation of this "literary dignitary" and her home in a former sixteenth-century inn is essentially truthful. (It is this mélange of the truthful and the false in his reportage that makes the detection of Truman's inventions impossible for an outsider, and almost impossible for a friend in a matter that does not touch him directly.) Even Truman's description of Baroness Blixen's "immense age" (she was seventy-three at the time) and of how her lips "twist in a sideways smile of rather paralytic contour" are, if not felicitous ("sideways" could have sufficed), within the scope of accuracy. But the description offended her, and "paralytic" was the detail she centered on as culpable. At that time she was in and out of the hospital and perhaps the word struck her as too close to her fears. Yet I would not be sure that her complaint to me revealed the whole source of her feelings.

Few people can admit, even to themselves, explicitly what it is that annoys them. To my eyes, Avedon's photographs of Isak

Dinesen should have been more upsetting to her than Truman's words, which also catch her charm. The photographs are more than unflattering; they are cruel. In the first the Baroness, dressed in a feathery black coat, her lips turned down, looks like a sated, rapacious bird. In the second her arms and hands are those of an Egyptian mummy. The third, a close-up of her face, is startlingly alive, the eyes liquidly dilated, but it seems someone else's face, it catches nothing of her age or her beauty. Years later, in 1976, Avedon published an unflattering and cruel photograph of Truman in his book *Portraits*. It looks like a rogues'-gallery shot of a resigned criminal. I was with Truman in his apartment when he received an original print of the photograph, sent in a box that photographic paper is packaged in. Truman was outraged. He asked if I had ever heard of such effrontery as Avedon's in sending it to him and declared that it was going straight into the garbage and down the incinerator. When I suggested that he give it to me instead, he put it back into the box, took it to his bedroom and closed the door on it.

But at the time of *Observations,* Truman believed, or pretended to believe, that there was nothing in the book to upset the Baroness. He wrote me shortly before I went to Denmark that he had heard she was "sore" about the book, and that he found this strange, but was sorry. After her death, Isak Dinesen's friends remembered the pain *Observations* had given her. In the book of tributes from seventy-six of her fellow writers and other artists, which Clara Svendsen edited for the Rungstedlund Foundation (an abbreviated version of which was published in the United States by Random House), no word from Truman is included. The frontispiece photograph is by Cecil Beaton.

Journalists writing about *In Cold Blood* often assume that Truman spent five years in Kansas working on it; but except for the first few months there, and several short trips back, he passed these years in Spain and in Verbier, Switzerland, where in 1961 he bought a small condominium apartment. *Very* small, a letter from him underlined, two rooms, a kitchen and bath; and, indeed, when I visited him and Jack there the next year, Truman slept on a pallet on the floor and gave me his bed, for there were only two narrow single beds, one in each room. This is his "chalet in Switzerland" in the articles of the same journalists; and it is from here, even more than from his rented houses in Spain, that from 1962 on Truman sent, as well as his letters to me, letters to Sandy who, tired of the uncertain life of an actor, had joined the editorial staff of *The New Yorker*. His job was in the checking department and he soon began to undertake certain tasks related to *In Cold Blood*. The magazine had agreed to serialize the entire book; the editors had found it the opposite of "unentertaining."

As I did, when I read the first three sections on a trip to Florida with Truman at the beginning of 1964. He had asked me to join him as a house guest of the Gardner Cowles' at their estate on Indian Creek Island; but when we arrived, driving down from New York in his Jaguar, we found that the Cowles had had to change their plans and we were the sole occupants of the place, except for the servants, Truman's new English bull, Charlie, and the Cowles' boxer, Bimbo.

The day after I read the typescript of the first three sections, Truman read aloud to me from his manuscript as much as he had finished of the fourth, up to the account of the trial. I was overwhelmed, but Truman was depressed. He had just learned by a long-distance telephone call to Kansas that Dick Hickock and Perry Smith, the convicted murderers of the Clutter family, had won the right to take their appeal all the way back to the Supreme Court a second time. The wait, and its possible endless extension, was beginning to tell on him. He had developed a twitch in his cheek; he blinked his eyes and wet his lips with his tongue, in a compulsive manner I had not seen before.

The strain had already begun at the time of the letter from Spain mentioned earlier. For several years his health problems had played a counterpoint to his work problems in his correspondence. It is hard for me to pin down now exactly what they were, as it was for him to decide then. At the beginning of 1961 he wrote that he had been felled by nicotine poisoning, which condition then brought on what he thought was a heart attack. He wound up in a London hospital. In March, he returned to Verbier; but in April, after a visit to Venice, he suffered a relapse and entered a hospital in Lausanne, where the doctors diagnosed his trouble as a crushed spinal nerve. Whatever his illness, all the doctors insisted that he stop smoking. He found this hard on his nerves and on his work; and, although I couldn't see it, he insisted that it had even changed his handwriting. By June, he was back in London to see English doctors again.

To the strain of his writing the book was added the strain of his waiting for the murderers to be executed. It is important to remember that he did not *choose* to write a book about killers. His original idea was to write about the effect of a violent crime on the inhabitants of the small town in which it occurred. It was by chance that the criminals were captured while he was on the spot and that he became involved with them and their fates. It had seemed just as likely as not when he first went to Kansas that the crime would remain unsolved. This chance capture gave him an opportunity to write a much more dramatic, a much bigger book. But it also put him into a situation he had not foreseen. There was no reason, other than a theoretical opposition to capital punishment, which neither Truman nor the law-enforcement officers he was involved with felt, for him to wish to save the lives of the two murderers, the full horror of whose crimes he had lived with more intensely and more intimately than any one other than the perpetrators themselves—and with a sensitivity unknown to them.

But it was not easy to be in the unasked-for position of wanting and waiting for the execution of two people whose deaths were necessary for the success of his project, a necessity he had not intended, but by which he would profit. And, ironically, it was again by chance that this "grim gamble,"* once he was in it, should be indefinitely drawn out. In the normal course of events Hickock and Smith, of whose criminal acts there was no question, would have been executed on the date first set, Friday, May 13, 1960. The strain, the anxiety-producing guilt, would have been bad enough in that case. But from that time on he was placed in the position of inescapably wanting and waiting for their demise.

He had almost returned from Verbier to Kansas in September 1962 to visit his friends, as he had come to refer to

Music for Chameleons.

them, before the hangman visited them. For although the word "friends" should be put in quotation marks, he had become closely involved with the two criminals, especially Perry Smith, as closely involved as a soldier with two prisoners trapped in a no-man's-land in a battle might be, on opposite sides but inexorably bound together. Then, at that point in the increasingly complex machinations of law enforcement, Hickock and Smith were granted their first right to appeal their conviction in the federal courts.

Despite this, when Truman had returned to the States at the beginning of 1963, he had not had the tics I saw a year later at Indian Creek Island. He was on his way to Kansas, via Alabama, and I rode with him as far as Georgia, where he dropped me off in Atlanta before he headed west. Earlier, we had stopped to spend the night with his aunt, his mother's sister whom I had met at the Park Avenue apartment at the time of his mother's death and who was living then in Charlotte, North Carolina.

People who say writers exaggerate the wildness of Southern family life don't know Southern family life. Animated discussions about various internecine family feuds went on cheerfully all the time we were in Charlotte, and among the assorted ironies was the fact that the two young male cousins who gave up their rooms to Truman and me had recently been in trouble with the police for beating up queers in a garage. There was a great deal of enthusiastic talk about money, for Truman was financing the educations of several of the relatives present. There were also a lot of compliments directed toward him for *Breakfast at Tiffany's* and I thought that his family was much more appreciative of his writing than my family was of mine until I was freed of my illusion when one of them added, "We particularly liked Audrey Hepburn."*

It was on this drive south that I witnessed one of Truman's more self-defeating posings to impress himself. In a small state liquor store, where the merchandise was on shelves separated from the customers by a counter, he asked for Justerini & Brooks scotch. The clerk replied that he had never heard of it

* A reaction foreshadowed in the novella itself when the narrator asks Holly to name a story that meant something to her and she chooses *Wuthering Heights*: "God, I cried buckets. I saw it ten times."

and Truman told him that he should have, for it was the only scotch worth drinking. Then, at our next stop, pouring us a drink of the J & B scotch I had bought, I saw that the name in small print was Justerini & Brooks and pointed out to Truman that the store had surely had it. All he had needed to do was to ask for it by that well-known abbreviation. But the next time we hit a state liquor store I overheard him playing the game again.

(A parenthetical note on the degree of literary appreciation I had at this time—not from my family but from my home town. After our stay on Indian Creek Island, I went to Atlanta to see my mother and the local book-review editors and bookstore managers. I was being published by Scribners at this time. They had brought out *The Warm Country*, my collection of short stories with E. M. Forster's introduction. In a few days they were releasing my autobiography about growing up in Atlanta, *Emblems of Conduct*. Their promotion department hoped the book would have a good sale there. The book editor at the *Atlanta Constitution* didn't know my other books, or, indeed, I suspect, my name; but he was an agreeable man. He became interested as we talked. Impressed by the fact that E. M. Forster had written about my work, he wanted to read some of my earlier books and called the leading bookstore to ask how many books by Donald Windham they had. "Three." "What are the titles?" "What do you mean, what are the titles? We have three copies of Windham's *Emblems of Conduct*.")

Despite Truman's tics and state of nervous exhaustion at Indian Creek Island that January, when Sandy went with him to Kansas the following October the physical symptoms of his strain had vanished. Or perhaps they were temporarily subdued by his manic social activities. From New York Sandy flew to Denver and joined Truman at the Brown Palace Hotel. Then they drove to Garden City, where Sandy was to do the semifinal checking on the first three sections of *In Cold Blood*, which *The New Yorker* had already set up in galleys. Truman was hosting a kind of traveling house party of friends, mainly people he had met during the work on his book. It included Alvin Dewey, the Kansas Bureau of Investigation agent central to the Clutter case, his wife, Marie, the widow of the deceased judge who had tried the case, and an old friend, a former *Harper's Bazaar* fiction editor. In Denver (where Truman picked up all his guests' hotel checks) and in Garden City, there were rounds of luncheon and dinner parties. At all of them Truman consumed a great deal of alcohol. Bloody marys before lunch. J & B or martinis before dinner. Every night he stayed up late drinking nightcaps with someone. He occasionally awoke with a hangover. But he recovered quickly. Unlike Clift, he seemed to be essentially unaffected by his drinking. While Sandy was questioning people, going over Dewey's file on the Clutter case, and checking passages in the book with a transcript of Perry Smith's confession, Truman was doing the work he had come to do, charming everyone in sight and, with the help of lawyers, his new friends and his cash, obtaining releases for the movie version of *In Cold Blood*. All this accomplished, he and Sandy left for Lansing. Truman had appointments at the prison there to talk with Hickock and Smith. When he introduced Sandy to them, separately, in a corridor, they responded with smiles and polite phrases, just like the guests at the luncheon and dinner parties.

Before Christmas, Truman returned to Verbier. From there he began to send Sandy reminders to keep his eye each Tuesday morning on the summary in the *N. Y. Times* of the Supreme Court's Monday decisions. The justices were once more due to grant or deny Hickock's and Smith's nth request for a review of their conviction. In January, his communications became increasingly urgent. The Court was to recess for the month of March. There were only a few Mondays left before then when they could hand down a decision. The minute Sandy saw the paper, each Tuesday, he was to cable "Writ denied," "Writ granted" or—if there was nothing—"Nothing."

The decision came on January 18. The writ was denied. Truman was in the highest state of tension he had been in. A new execution date was set for February 18. Having decided that he could, as he wished, avoid the hanging, Truman arranged for Sandy to talk with Alvin Dewey that morning, then to cable Switzerland. Truman himself would already have been on the telephone to Dewey. On February 7, the Supreme Court granted another stay of execution.

On the eighteenth, Truman wrote that he had finished the

final section of the book, all except for an inevitably missing page or two. He was exhausted and coming home.

Hickock and Smith were hanged shortly after midnight on the morning of April 14. Sandy read a small item in the *N. Y. Times* that morning as we were having breakfast. Truman was in New York and when we had talked to him a few days before he had not mentioned a possible execution. He expected another postponement. Sandy called his apartment. Jack answered. Truman had flown to Kansas at the last minute. Perry and Dick had asked him to come.

That evening, back in New York, Truman telephoned. When Perry had gone up to the gallows he had stopped in front of Truman, kissed him, and said "Adios, amigo." The ritual of the execution, Truman said, had been like a high-school graduation. Each of the condemned was left hanging for twenty minutes. After Perry was dead and taken away, the warden came up to Truman and gave him an envelope, saying, "Mr. Smith wanted you to have this." It contained all the money Truman had sent Perry over the last five years. When he reached this point in his story, he burst into tears and had to hang up.

$\cdot$ 7 $\cdot$

In Cold Blood is a singular achievement. It is, for me, Capote's best book. It is also his most conventional. The form is classic. His triumph is the accuracy of his imaginative invention, the instinctive truths he found in himself, which enabled him to create convincingly and movingly within the confines of the known facts the inner workings of his major characters, especially of the killer Perry Smith, and to pare down to what was interesting and capable of being dramatically exaggerated the observable facts about the minor ones.

But, and although this shouldn't have surprised me it did, it was what he hadn't done, not what he had done, that Truman claimed to have done.

In my early teens I worked in a drugstore. From among the periodicals that were displayed in a long rack near the front door, I read the various weekly *True Detective* magazines that were staple publications of the 1930s. I would have recognized the form Truman was using, extended to a length and raised to a height it had never achieved before, as the routine presentation of these publications—author absent, behind the narrative, law enforcers and criminals forward—even if I hadn't seen a room stacked with old copies of these magazines in Truman's house at Bridgehampton when he was working on his book. But his maneuver was to announce that he had invented a wholly new form, never known before: the nonfiction novel.

Admittedly, since his object was to attract publicity and to sell his book, his maneuver was smart. The claim was no good; but as Monty saw, Truman's charm, and now not only his charm but also his passionate rationalization, convinced. Endless people who should have known better discussed pro and con the authenticity of his claim, the suitability of the name he had given his "new" form. It didn't matter that a few sensible people pointed out, most often with admiration, just what he had done; their words were drowned in the chatter.

As if it wasn't enough to have this claim accepted as a subject for public debate, he went further. He announced that every word he had written in his nonfiction novel was factually true. How could this be of events he had not witnessed? Easily, he said. After they were captured, Hickock and Smith were not allowed to be alone together: but he, and only he, had the confidences of both of them. He arrived at the facts by discounting their stories when they differed and crediting them when they were the same. His truth was the unagreed-upon versions they both told him. In such statements he gave any reader who wanted to doubt his nonfiction claim the clue to lead him through the maze of scenes in the book not corroborated by official records. The only check on Truman's factualness was Dick and Perry. *In Cold Blood* couldn't be and wasn't published until Dick and Perry were dead. When the book came out, the only living authority for the factualness of much of the narrative was Truman himself. It was a perfect setup for his kind of invention.

Once again, his claim was accepted as a subject for serious discussion. But the more material for publicity, the better. With the boldness that was his second nature, he went still further. Questioned as to how his recollection of conversations could be accurate when he did not use a tape recorder or make notes, he replied with a Tom Swift fantasy. He had trained himself over the years, being read to and later writing down what he heard, until he had achieved ninety-odd (he could not remember the exact figure from one interview to the next) percent of perfect memory. This claim was nearer to home and more journalists resisted it than had the earlier ones, but by and large their objections were gnats spat out by the swallowers of whales. I don't remember hearing a single voice raised to point out that these web-spinnings were the equivalent of the earlier ones, now admitted by him to be false, of making a living by painting flowers on glass, tap dancing on a riverboat, ghostwriting politicians' speeches.

No wonder Truman's widening confidence in what he could

get by with grew. No wonder he felt an urge to see how far he could go. And no wonder his frail respect for the distinction between truth and invention became even frailer.

All this did not affect the achievement of his book, whatever effect it had on the book's sales, but its greatest effect was to be on Truman himself.

In Cold Blood was the publishing event of the year. One of the few openly hostile reviews was by Stanley Kauffmann in *The New Republic*. He dismissed the book as "residually shallow." His attack, when I read it, struck me as answerable on every point, even though too sneering to answer. Then, as I was leaving my apartment to go to meet Truman, I returned and wrote a one-sentence letter to the editor: "Stanley Kauffmann has green eyes."

I was delighted when *The New Republic* printed my communication. Truman didn't need my defense, but out of friendship I wanted to defend him against what I considered an unjust attack. My impetus, however, was not wholly altruistic. The year before, Kauffmann had written an equally sneering review of my novel *Two People*. ("In this book destined to wither in a season . . .") I didn't know Kauffmann, but I didn't wish him well. I certainly didn't wish to flatter him. It was a while later that I realized this was what I had done. I knew *Othello;* I didn't, however, know the definition of *jealousy*. It had to be pointed out to me that people are jealous of what they have and fear losing. I certainly had not meant to suggest that Kauffmann possessed anything to lose, or indeed anything other than envy.

My confusion of jealousy and envy was like my confusion of envy and covetousness. They seemed the same sin viewed from different viewpoints until I understood that you envy people and covet objects. Thinking of how I believed in the early days that Truman wanted to make me envy him in order to make me like him, I asked myself if he was envious or covetous. I didn't feel that he envied people for their good fortunes, their having possessions he didn't have; he rather liked them for it; but I did feel that he coveted their possessions and wanted to have for himself the subject matter of their stories, the friendship of their friends, their attachments, their antipathies. He didn't appear to worry about losing what he had. Indeed, he often appeared not to value what he had because he had it. But he did seem to want to possess what others had, because they had it.

When I wrote earlier that I interpreted his dissatisfaction with his subject matter to mean that he had come to feel the subject matter wasn't his and therefore didn't repay the skill he devoted to it, I had in mind the derivativeness of his early stories. In 1950, before I left for Europe, I gave Truman a copy of *The Dog Star*. He read it on the freighter he and Jack took to Naples. The first afternoon he was in Taormina, he read me "A Diamond Guitar," a story he had written on the crossing. The events and characters of "A Diamond Guitar" are not taken from *The Dog Star*. No one else would be likely to recognize the relation between the two works. But the assembled properties of his story come from my novel: the emblematic guitar, passed on as an inheritance; the glass jewels; the blondness of the guitar player; the settings—a prison farm, a creek in the woods; the repeated images of sunlight on a woman's hair. I didn't mention my recognition to Truman. But I thought about it. It corroborated my earlier impression that the inspiration for his writing was not experience but reading, an impression easy for anyone to get who reads Eudora Welty's "Why I Live at the P. O." (1941), then Capote's "My Side of the Matter" (1945), etc. *

Before *In Cold Blood* was published, Truman established in the minds of certain key individuals that the book was going to earn two million dollars. Even when *In Cold Blood* was only half finished, Mark Schorer, not a promotion copy writer but an academic critic, wrote in his introduction to Capote's *Selected Writings* that *In Cold Blood* was going to be Capote's most remarkable and exciting change as a writer. I didn't know Truman when he was selling his early stories, but he must, even then, have used this technique of mesmerizing people into believing what a sensation they would make. Given the stories, how did he bring it

---

*Carson McCullers continued her accusations of Truman's poachings. "She thought that one passage in particular in *The Grass Harp* had a striking affinity in meaning, imagery and syntax to her own 'A Tree. A Rock. A Cloud.'" But: "Even Carson's phrase 'A Tree. A Rock. A Cloud.' was taken from Thomas Wolfe's 'A Leaf, A Stone, A Door,' whether consciously or unconsciously. It was fairly ridiculous, people thought, that she reacted so strongly to someone's 'poaching' from her—even if he had—when she herself had borrowed." Virginia Spencer Carr, *The Lonely Hunter*.

off? How did he convince himself and others? In later years he elaborated a scenario about how from an early age he had trained himself to write. In truth, I think that from an early age he trained himself in the *a-priori* rejection of reality and the setting up of his desired alternative to it.

Herbart, in his book on Gide, says that Gide triumphed as an artist because he had every fault it takes to end in sterility and despair; for each fault he found an antidote of equal magnitude, which allowed his work to blossom forth. Truman's "fault" from an early age must have been that he was aware with intense, painful sensitivity of the reality around him and opposed it. This fault—if that is what it is—is not something aside from his virtues as a writer, however great or small they may be; it forms the single stream which fed what he was and what he said; his virtues as a writer are part and parcel of the same sensitivity and opposition. His passion for friendship must have been a longing for the small islands of repose that friendship gave him in the swirling battles of this conflict. His David challenge to the Goliath of reality took place in daily life as well as in daydreams, for what he wanted was from the real world. The odds against his getting it were the source of his boldness and invention. The resulting audacity elicited belief as well as admiration—especially from those who did not know what was going on. This mesmerism must have already been working for him in 1945, just as it was still working for him in 1965. And there seemed no reason then for it not to go on working for him indefinitely. However, to battle reality you must remain in the ring with it; you must not kayo it. The bout is one that you are not supposed to win, and in the rational course of events it is one that you cannot win. But the world was leading Truman to believe that he could win it. And he was praying to win it, even while he was quoting Saint Thérèse's "More tears are shed over answered prayers than unanswered ones."*

---

*Truman uses indiscriminately the names of the French saint, Thérèse, and the Spanish, Theresa. None of the Catholic scholars I have approached has been able to find this quotation attributed to either.

· 8 ·

When I saw Truman in New York it was nearly always without Jack. He would be in Philadelphia, visiting relatives; or on Long Island, after Truman bought his houses there; or in Verbier, skiing. This was the situation not merely with me but with all of Truman's acquaintances. Some of them had never even met Jack. According to Truman, he and Jack got along perfectly well in New York so long as there were only the two of them, but that Jack became impossible as soon as a third person joined them.

Even though Jack was almost never with Truman in New York, one or another of the animals usually was. Kelly had belonged originally to Jack, I believe; Truman, however, was equally fond of him. And equally indulgent. Neither of them would discipline him to accept being on a leash; whenever I walked him in Taormina I had to face that he would strain ahead and choke himself. The other dogs were Truman's. He lavished affection on them and spoiled them as he would like to have been spoiled as a child. Bunkie was calmer about the leash, but he had an uncontrolled erotic attraction to the human leg. Charlie was better behaved in both these respects, but Truman made no effort to curb his fury to chew up whatever was chewable. When he was around I learned to keep a sharp eye on any shirt or shoe of mine his jaws could reach.

Out of fondness for Truman, I was fond of Bunkie and Charlie; but I liked Kelly best. Aside from his predilection for nipping other dogs and strangers, he harmed nothing but himself. And I knew him best. He was with Truman and Jack wherever they were from 1950 until he died at the beginning of 1962, predeceased a year earlier by the younger Bunkie.

One of my memories of Kelly is from the summer of 1957 at

Sailaway, a house Truman and Oliver Smith were renting in Bridgehampton. His coat had turned salt-and-pepper gray; he had developed cataracts on both eyes—milky white cataracts, like the one Tennessee had on his left eye when I first knew him. In the rented house he had memorized the placement of the furniture and made his way around the rooms with few hesitations. Outdoors, he depended on the sharpness of his hearing for guidance. He stuck close to whoever was walking him, never straining ahead now, and moved cautiously when he was let off the leash. But on the deserted extent of the seashore he gained confidence. One day, as he was trotting along he tripped over a low rope stretched tight over the beach a few inches above the sand. He stopped in frightened bewilderment and, while the group of us were momentarily silent, turned his head helplessly this way and that, not daring to move his feet, a pale ghost of his former aggressiveness.

It was Charlie, Truman's second English bull, who accompanied him and me to Palm Springs in January 1968. For three years running, while Jack was in Switzerland, skiing, and Sandy in Florida with his mother, Truman and I had spent the Christmas holidays together at his studio in Bridgehampton. This trip to California was more complicated. Early in December, Truman had decided to have his face lifted. I tried to dissuade him, but when he insisted that he knew what he was doing and that I was the only person he was telling about the operation, I agreed to accompany him to Palm Springs after the holidays while he was recuperating.

Twice, the week before Christmas, I went to see him in the hospital. After the bandage was removed, he had black eyes but no other visible ill effects, and the day after he was dismissed, wearing dark glasses, he drove us to Bridgehampton. An hour after our arrival, Truman, who was upstairs, called that his portable TV wasn't where it should be. Then he came down and looked in the bedroom; the drawers of the chest and the hangers in the closet were half empty. Many of his shirts and sweaters were gone, and his Browning automatic. The selection had been carefully made to conceal that the house had been burglarized; only one typewriter was taken from a room where there were two, several portable radios were left. Truman got on the telephone to neighbors, caretaker service, the police. Then he decided to have a drink. All the liquor was gone from both houses. We drove to the liquor store without waiting for the police.*

Charlie suffered from bronchitis. A grill had been installed behind the front seat of Truman's new automobile, a station wagon, to keep him and Truman's white-chested black kitten, Happy, in the rear section during our drive west. On our return to Manhattan, Truman's luggage slid forward and knocked the grill down. Charlie spent the trip, as was his habit, with his feet on the backrest and his face snorting beside mine, trying to climb over into the front seat. After we were back, the grill was replaced; but I came down with what Truman would call "walking pneumonia." I stayed in the house for two days fortifying myself with Alka-Seltzer, vitamin C and aspirin before I felt well enough to travel.

Sandy's and my financial states, as well as Truman's, had improved in the previous years. We had moved from a small apartment on Eightieth Street to a large one on Central Park South at the same time that Truman had transferred his main residence from the ground floor of Oliver Smith's house on Willow Street in Brooklyn Heights to a tower apartment at United Nations Plaza. I stayed with him the night before our departure and we left before dawn. At the end of the first day I suffered a relapse. The second night, through the manager of our motel, Truman found a doctor for me. He said I had bronchitis, gave me an injection and a prescription. For two days I lived mainly on pills and cough syrup. On New Year's, I felt well

---

*The police solved the burglary because they were concerned about the theft of the gun. Truman, in interviews and articles, has given increasingly good versions of what happened. The one I like best was in Andy Warhol's *Interview* in 1979. He returns to Bridgehampton after having started for California. As he approaches the studio, various of his possessions are strewn along the lane leading to it. "When I got to the house the thieves had been there with a moving van and simply stripped the place. They'd taken the refrigerator and washing machine and the furniture. Everything. I called the police. While I was waiting for the police I saw lying on the ground a camera. I picked it up. It was one of those cheap little instamatic cameras that somebody had left at my house accidentally during the summer. It was tucked in a drawer and I'd never thought anything about it. But I looked at it and I noticed that all of the films had been used up. When the police arrived I handed them the camera. On a hunch, the police developed the film and lo and behold the thieves had taken photographs of themselves hauling away all of my furniture. They were drinking my liquor and smiling and laughing and holding bottles of whiskey and going, 'Gurgle, gurgle, gurgle.'"

enough to join Truman for a J & B before dinner at our motel outside Dallas. Truman, although he looked hardly any different to me, discounting the unnatural smoothness about his eyes, had recovered from his operation.

We rose early each morning, stopped only briefly for lunch, and averaged five hundred miles a day. As Truman drove, we talked and listened to the Good Guys radio station. I handed him various pairs of his rainbow assortment of tinted glasses with the changes of the daylight; I lit him cigarettes. He sometimes drove steadily from lunch until we stopped for the night at one or another chain motel. Our routine on arrival was always the same. I checked in, got the keys to both rooms and opened the doors. Then Truman rushed to lock Happy in the bathroom of one, his, and to pee in the bathroom of the other, mine.

The house Truman had rented was in the middle of Palm Springs. The furnishings were chichi. Every surface was covered with knickknacks, antique cups and saucers, china animals, iron figurines, glass, faience, and silver ashtrays. But there was no table in my bedroom until I found a folding dinner tray and set it up to hold my typewriter. The yard, with its heated pool and citrus trees, was surrounded by high walls. Beyond, all you could see was the sky and the tops of mountains. It was a perfect setup for working, especially as no one Truman knew was there.

From my letters to Sandy: "It is apparently for the attendants at the Spa that T. has brought his large wardrobe: one day all in yellow, one day all in brown, he drives us there, we enter the lobby and cross to the health section with its steam rooms and masseurs. Afterward, we get in the car and drive home. For supper we return to the Spa dining room. That is the height of the social whirl. He is on the telephone often, however, to New York, arranging dinner parties for the opening night of the revival of *House of Flowers*. Happy disappears for the main part of the day. 'I'm sure he's safe,' I say. 'Yes, but I brought him here for *company*,' T. replies. We go to bed by eight or nine. I'm up by seven and work until ten."

But Truman wasn't working. He slept late. When he retired to his room in the afternoon for what was supposed to be his work hour, he would carry a bottle of wine with him. Then I would hear him on the telephone to New York or Los Angeles, trying to calm Harold Arlen's apprehensions about the *House of Flowers* revival; repeating to everyone else, like a chant, that all connected with the revival agreed it was so great it would run two to five years and that the Theatre de Lys was planning to change its name to House of Flowers; or informing his agent that a movie reviewer, from whom he had received a letter saying that although she had been upset by the film of *In Cold Blood* when she first saw it she now thought it very good, had sent him a telegram saying that she was naming it the best film of the year.

This would go on until we met for drinks. Truman was drinking an awful lot: a bloody mary before lunch, followed by three or four large vodkas, then wine. Before dinner, about a bottle of white wine (instead of "early drinks"), then four or five vodkas at the house, and two or three more at the restaurant. The daytime drinking never seemed to affect him, although it had bothered me on the trip when he would pour three or four slugs of vodka into his water glass in the roadside restaurants we stopped at, eat a tiny lunch, then get behind the wheel again.

In Palm Springs, instead of writing he talked about the writing he was going to do. He told me his new novel would be twice as long as *Remembrance of Things Past*—the protagonist, he confided, would not appear until seven hundred pages into the book—talk that only someone who knew nothing about him or about writing could believe. By that time, he had become a regular guest on all the biggest TV talk shows. He was recognized, when he walked Charlie, by the other travelers and the managers of the motels we stopped in. It was due to this recognition that he was able to get a good doctor for me in Greenville, South Carolina. In Palm Springs I became aware of another, and less fortunate, effect of his success with the TV public. These shows were either taped or rerun; consequently, he could see himself on the screen as I had felt he imagined seeing himself through my eyes in the early days. What he wanted to see and hear played back to him had increasingly less and less to do with reality; and he began to talk to me as though I knew no more about him, and was no more to him, than another guest on one of the talk shows.

The change may seem slight but it was a progression, not only from the time when I first knew him and was frequently unaware which of his stories were fact and which fiction—after all, he could have known Gide more easily than I could; one hundred night-flying moths might have lit on his window screen—but even from the Willow Street days when, with Sandy and me in attendance, he showed a journalist from Kansas through Oliver's house, floor by floor, describing how he, Truman, had restored and furnished it, although he was aware we knew that the house and all the furnishings above the ground floor were Oliver's. Such stories were told in front of us, but not to us. Now he was telling me untruths which, although they might deceive a TV audience, could only disconcert me, since I knew beforehand, or would know immediately afterward, that they were lies.

In New York, when he left the hospital, I discovered that everybody at Random House and on Long Island, even his most casual acquaintances, had been told all about his "eye job." He would discuss it with them in front of me, then again insist that they didn't know about it. In Palm Springs when his bill for the operation came he said, "Well, this is more than I thought it would be." He had told me that a woman friend of mine who had had the same operation couldn't have afforded his doctor because he charged five thousand dollars, so I asked how much the bill was. "I thought it would be two thousand and it's four thousand." Then he left the bill lying on the counter by the kitchen telephone. It was for one thousand. The previous year in Bridgehampton, he had shown me the taxwise contract his lawyer had worked out for the payment of his royalties from *In Cold Blood* and of the unprecedented advance he was getting for his upcoming books, $750,000 worth of stocks held in trust, from which he received the income. He had shown it to me without bragging, with the straightforward enjoyment of his success I was used to. So why these peanut fantasies? Some of his other fantastications were easier to understand. One morning a list of the ten best-dressed men in America was published in the newspaper we both read. It didn't include Truman's name, although it did that of one or more of his friends. As we were driving to the Spa, he said, "Well, at last they've put me on the list of the ten best-dressed men in America. Not that I shouldn't have been on it for years."*

Sometimes I challenged his more obvious wallowings in the imaginary, not on matters like these but on ones that touched me. I wanted to draw him back closer and he was usually willing to laugh at himself and his fabrications. But his attitude didn't change. It was during one of these conversations, when I corrected him about where I had met Melton, that he said I might be right, but that it was better his way, I *should have* met Melton where he said, and he remembered things the way they should have been.

Sometimes, also, he bragged, to me and in front of me, in the brash manner he was beginning to use on the talk shows— in contrast to his early sensitivity to other people, his care not to score at their expense. I note this, like the above, not because it was so unpleasant but because it was so unusual. One day at the Spa when the woman at the desk was returning the valuables we had checked, Truman took my wallet and handed me his. I pointed out his mistake. As he took his wallet, he chuckled to the woman, "And, believe you me, it's got a lot more in it."

My certainty that Happy was all right when he disappeared was optimistic. One morning he turned up covered in blood, one eye swollen and filled with pus, one ear ripped, raw tears in his fur—mewing pitifully. Truman turned away in horror. I held Happy while he telephoned the veterinarian. On the drive to the clinic he wouldn't look at the cat. When we arrived he made me

---

*The pattern is, perhaps, self-evident. In 1950, at Harry's Bar in Venice, Truman was intrigued by two fiftyish ladies at the next table. Their hands were kissed by everyone who came up to speak to them. "Who are those two women?" he asked the waiter. Leaning toward us, the man whispered, "The one on the right is the Queen of Greece, the one on the left is the Queen of Rumania." I waited to see how Truman would tell this. He never mentioned it.

Oscar Wilde recognized the pattern. In Gide's 1902 memoir of Wilde, he recounts Wilde's tale of a man who was loved in his village because each evening when the laborers returned from work he told them fabulous stories of what he had done that day, of having seen a faun in a wood playing a flute, of having watched sirens at the water's edge combing their hair. One day, taking a walk, he came upon three sirens on the seashore combing their green hair with a golden comb and, farther on, a faun playing a flute to a circle of dancing wood spirits. That evening when the villagers asked, as they did each evening, "What did you see today?" he answered, "I saw nothing at all."

carry Happy inside and give him to the attendant before he came to talk to the doctor. And as long as Happy was there he had me call and relay to him the news I was told, while he stood by twisting his hands.

Truman had invited me to stay in Palm Springs until Lee Radziwill came to join him the middle of the month to watch a broadcast of the TV play of *Laura* he had adapted for her. When she cancelled her visit because one of her children was ill and I didn't want to stay longer, he invited Cecil Beaton. Cecil arrived a couple of days before I left. While the two of us were in Palm Springs, Truman's megalomania reached a new degree.

At dinner in a candlelit restaurant Cecil's first night there, Truman went on about how he had done everything right in regard to the movie of *In Cold Blood,* how the picture had cost two million to make, "couldn't possibly, possibly" earn less than twenty-eight million, and he owned a third of it. In passing he mused, "I wonder who's paying for all those ads for *Closely Watched Trains.* They have a big one every day." I suggested that it was the distributors, who hoped to get a big national distribution. "Look! I'm an expert on these things. I know exactly how much money is available for these things, and *they* don't have that kind of money." Cecil lamented that Aubrey's *Brief Lives* had been a flop on Broadway. I said it didn't have good promotion. "What d'ya mean?" Truman objected. "They had a full-page ad in the *N. Y. Times!*" I started to say that he knows better than anyone else that promotion isn't paid advertising, but he drowned me out, protesting, "No, no, no!" And then went on to repeat what I had been saying, plus that if you want to do something, *something important, naturally,* and you can't get at least five million dollars' worth of free publicity, then you'd better just forget it and not try to do it *at all.* And that there's only *one person in the world* who can do it, and do you know who that is? (Holding his hand straight out in front of him and pointing his finger back at himself:) "Me, me!" (Tapping himself on the forehead and raising his voice:) "Yours truly!" This was after Cecil and I had both started eating our dinners and Truman was still drinking and chain-smoking, just before he ate his small portion of meat, the one point every day when he got that way, the point at which one night on our trip he had gone on about all the millions he was going to leave Jack and would Jack, so spoiled and unrealistic, so unlike him, do something foolish with it, the night he said to me, "I live in reality. Jack doesn't and hasn't for twenty years." And as Cecil pointed out the next day, such scenes went as quickly as they came: an hour later at the house he was his usual self, quiet and sweet.

TWO

.

"Truth is no Apollo Belvedere . . ."

—Marianne Moore,
"In the Days of Prismatic Colour"

· 9 ·

The period I originally intended to cover in my memoir using Truman's letters was past by the beginning of 1970 when, needing a place to stay alone during a personal crisis, I telephoned him in California. He said I could stay in the United Nations Plaza apartment and arranged for the concierge to give me the key.

To divert my mind, I took with me a book in Italian by Aldo Palazzeschi. It was partly in order to read Palazzeschi that I had taught myself Italian; and in Rome, in 1967, when he was eighty-two years old, I had met him.* We had become friends and I hoped to get more of his works published here. William Maxwell at *The New Yorker* had suggested that I make a rough English version of the pieces in *Stampe dell'800,* Palazzeschi's stories of his childhood in Florence at the end of the last century, that I thought the magazine could publish, and while at Truman's apartment I set out to do this.

The rooms at United Nations Plaza were almost as full of knickknacks as those of the rented house in Palm Springs. They had the same decorator touch. On the wall over the living-room couch there hung a mosque window—a wooden frame with panes of colored mirrors—a gift, Truman said, from the Shah of Persia. Sandy and I had seen it in an antique shop in our neighborhood shortly before he acquired it. Still, the United Nations Plaza apartment was more personal than the Palm Springs house. All of the hundred-or-so books filling the cases in the

---

*Palazzeschi was solitary, not because he had outlived his friendships but his friends. Like Gide, he remained creative to the end. Between the time I met him and his death at 89, in 1974, he published three youthful short novels and two collections of new poetry. His masterpiece, *The Sisters Materassi,* appeared in 1934. He gave me a copy of the original edition of his first novel, *Riflessi,* which he had published himself in 1908: Editore (publisher) Cesare Blanc (his cat).

library-dining room were by Truman, in multiple copies of his various world-wide editions. The walls and tables were clustered with Kodachrome snapshots of him with the rich friends he was proud of knowing, William and "Babe" Paley (he had dedicated *The Muses Are Heard* to Mrs. Paley), Lee Radziwill, etc.

Looking for some paper in the drawer of the table where I had put my typewriter, I found a stack of manuscript. It was apparently part of his new novel, *Answered Prayers*—some thirty or forty pages of sexually explicit anecdotes about writers, one about a stud fucking "the first lady of letters in America," another about a male whore's visit to "a chunky, paunchy, booze-puffed runt" who "some ten years earlier . . . was the most ac-claimed American playwright."

Reading the manuscript was a shock. Especially those pages describing the playwright at the end of a two-day drunk in a Hotel Plaza suite filled with wet dog shit and drying dog piss. I was staying in Jack's room, as Truman had suggested I do, and the table was one Jack used. I tried to imagine what he would have said to Truman after reading what I had read, and what words would have come from the editors at Random House or whoever else might have read it.

The shock these pages gave me came less from the picture they offered of their subjects than from the impression they left of their author. Despite its clear intention, the portrait of the playwright, with its inclusion of biographical facts and incidents from newspaper clippings about Tennessee, exhibited no obser-vation of, or insight into, Tennessee's character. But it was the crassness of the jokes and of the writing that upset me. Indeed, I wondered if this could really be a part of Truman's novel or if I hadn't stumbled on early discards or on something he had written as a joke to amuse Jack by demonstrating what a low parody of a Jacqueline Susann best-seller he could turn out if he wanted to.

As unlikely as it seemed, Truman was jealous of Jacqueline Susann. He felt about her as Gore had felt about him. She had taken over, or at least he felt that she had taken over, his place on the best-seller lists. She had proved that he was not the one person in the world who could get a million dollars' worth of free publicity. He made cracks about her on various TV talk

Truman and Don, Piazza San Marco, July, 1948

Don and Sandy, Florence, April, 1948
(*Photograph by Tennessee Williams*)

Gore, Truman and Tennessee, New York, October, 1948
(Photograph by Jo Healy)

Tennessee in his salad days, Provincetown
(Collection of Fritz Bultman)

Monty, New York, 1948
(Photograph by Karl Bissinger)

André Gide, Greek Theater, Taormina, April 1950

With Frank Merlo, Donald Windham, Maria Britneva and Sandy
Campbell, New York, December, 1948

Tennessee, Italy, 1948

Truman: "He liked people and wanted to be liked; he charmed."
(Photograph by Fred Melton)

shows. I knew this, but it had not occurred to me that he considered her *his* competition, that he coveted *her* subject matter, that he thought "I could do that better" about *her* work.

But although I wondered if what I had read had been written as a joke, I didn't quite believe it. I decided that if Truman offered me the manuscript to read I would tell him what I felt. The problem involved was one I had thought about when he advised me to write a *roman à clef* about Tennessee. I hadn't dismissed his suggestion without examining it. I could tell him *why* I thought that whatever momentary excitement and advantage it might produce would vanish as surely as though it were written in disappearing ink. But this conversation was not to take place.

Not because there had been any diminution in our friendship after Palm Springs. It was to Truman, and to no one else, I had turned in my difficulty. But he was seldom in New York. He was spending less and less time with Jack, either here or in Europe, and more and more time with new acquaintances in California. These new acquaintances were people who didn't care if he was working. People who couldn't question the reality he presented to them. People who treated him as a celebrity into whose intimacy they were privileged to enter. When he talked about them, it was in boasting stories of their sexual attractiveness, described in salacious physical detail, an entirely new note with him—a parallel to the dirty-story quality of the pages I had read.

Those pages were in my mind at the end of the year, when for the only time I can remember Truman asked to be invited to our apartment to meet someone. Robert Buckingham, the policeman who for many years had been the friend of E. M. Forster, and Buckingham's wife, May, were in New York. Forster had taken me to the Buckinghams' house in London for dinner in 1950; I had eaten lunch with May in Cambridge several times later on when I was visiting Forster there; and in June Sandy and I had been at the Buckinghams' house in Coventry for Forster's funeral. Truman had never met Forster, but he said that he would like to meet the Buckinghams anyway. So not without some misgivings, I included him among the people we invited to dinner with them. Aside from the pieces I had read at the

United Nations Plaza apartment, I had heard Truman say, and had read in interviews, that he was putting into his novel all the scandal that existed about everyone in the literary life of our time, and it inevitably crossed my mind that a desire to "check out" the Buckinghams for his book might be behind his desire to meet them.

The period I originally intended to cover in my memoir had ended by the early 1970s because from then on I received few written communications from Truman, only an occasional postcard when he was traveling. There were no longer interests in common for him to write me about the new friends he was increasingly absorbed in. How many of them were there? Two, three? It was hard for me to tell these California air-conditioning repairmen, bank clerks, etc. apart. I saw none of them and the stories about all of them were the same. They were married, fathers, physically attractive, and ready to leave their wives and children for Truman. I pictured them as the male members of Truman's TV audience, as seen in their own smoking-room stories. However many of them there were in California, I met the pivotal New York one, Johnny, shortly after he appeared. On Mother's Day weekend in 1974, Truman and he came to see Sandy and me at the house Sandy had bought on Fire Island.

We met them at the ferry dock in Sayville. Truman arrived first, coming from the parking lot. Johnny followed. In each hand he carried a large black suitcase. (Sandy, moving one of them later, thought it was heavy enough to be filled with liquor bottles, but Truman said it contained his financial records that Johnny was straightening out.) In between the suitcases walked a squat figure in clothes too tight and too youthful for their middle-aged wearer, topped by a fleshy face, its pallor emphasized by badly dyed hair, cut in a clumsy imitation of a rock singer's.

The weekend was as big a shock as the pages of *Answered Prayers*. Aside from Johnny's appearance, he lacked any mental traits that I could connect with what I knew Truman to be interested in. The only link between them seemed to be pathological. Johnny was from Long Island and still living with his wife and children, but on this weekend, a sort of double-header which combined Mother's Day with his daughter's sixteenth birthday,

Truman was in possession. He watched Johnny with an obsessed nervousness, but without pleasure, like a man staring at a mirage. The effort seemed to drain him. He slept until noon on Saturday and Sunday; he got up only in time to have a bloody mary or a screwdriver before lunch; then he was on the telephone orchestrating and hearing about the daughter's birthday party (which he was paying for): a trip to Manhattan in a Carey Cadillac with another teenaged girl for dinner at Orsini's, seats for *Irene,* and a Carey Cadillac home. While he was on the telephone about these matters, he stayed in his ankle-length red nightshirt; he didn't dress; he didn't go to the beach. After that, he took a nap until drinks at six. He dressed then and, like an actor onstage, charmed our neighbors, who had been invited over; to Sandy and me he was considerate, helping us with the dishes after each meal, while Johnny lounged around studying the manual of instructions for a new camera he had been given. But Truman didn't seem to enjoy being with us, despite his smiles and laughter, any more than he did with Johnny. His presence was pale; his relation to his surroundings oblique. He twitched until he had a drink; and he told with apparent satisfaction that when he had been ill in California the year before, in a coma, the doctors said he had moaned, "Oh, let me go, let me go!"

Sunday evening we all returned to the city in Truman's Buick. Johnny drove. It was the first time I had known Truman to let someone else take the wheel of one of his cars when he was in it; and as the drab Long Island throughways passed, I thought, as great as their differences were, his state was beginning to resemble Monty's and Tennessee's; his contrast to their misery was fading.

· 10 ·

Montgomery Clift had died of a coronary occlusion in July 1966. After his funeral at St. James's Episcopal Church on Madison Avenue (where we were to go the next October to Carson McCullers's funeral), Sandy and I ate lunch at the Plaza Hotel. We had sometimes accompanied Monty there in the early days to the travel agent he used, and it seemed an appropriate place to have our wake.

The friendship between us had gone on, however tenuously, until the end. Monty came to our Eightieth Street apartment on several occasions for dinner. Each time he was not drinking, although once I found him in the kitchen staring at the liquor bottles. My last glimpse of him was in the block where we lived. I was coming out of our building and caught sight of him walking along the sidewalk. Having undergone operations for cataracts, he was wearing steel-rimmed glasses; with both hands he held a slip of paper before his eyes. He was staring at it so intently that he seemed in character as a bewildered émigré professor. I instinctively looked around to see if a camera was following, and he went on down the street without my having called his name. A month before his death, later that year, on his way home from making his last movie, in Germany, he sent us a postcard (of Rodin's "The Kiss"), from England, saying that he hoped to see us when he was in New York.

Nine years later, in 1975, Tennessee, who had moved me in the early 1940s because he believed he was dying, was very much alive and complaining in his *Memoirs* that he suffered from the curse of longevity.

What kind of picture did Tennessee think he was giving of himself in the *Memoirs*? Trying to disarm the reader against its sordid indiscretions, he jocosely protests that he is "knocking out" this "thing" for money. It is easy to imagine that the impetus for the book came when his agent said to him, "Look, you give away all this material to interviewers and *they* make money out of it. Why not get it for yourself?" Large sections of the book are patched together from those interviewers' articles, which Tennessee invariably denounced when they appeared. Others read as though they have been dictated and sloppily transcribed. But aside from the writing, what did Tennessee, so touchy about every word anyone else says about him, think he was saying about himself? His account of his cruelty toward Frank Merlo in the last year of Merlo's life is so upsetting to read that compared to it Truman's version of the same events in his *Answered Prayers* excerpt is a Pollyanna whitewash.

One of the most unpleasant passages is his portrait of Jo Healy. She had been Tennessee's friend and admirer since 1940, when she was switchboard operator at the Theatre Guild at the time of the abortive production of *Battle of Angels*. Her attachment to him had not lessened in the intervening years before his success. Since then, for a decade she had undertaken the task of visiting his sister in the nursing home where she lived near New York and bringing her to the city when Tennessee wanted to see her. She often irritated me by urging me to be friends again with him. Her blind devotion could be annoying. Withal, she was defenseless and a perfect target for his compulsion to inflict pain. Calling her Miss Nameless, he describes her as an "Irish biddy, deep in her cups and mean as a rattler" (two impossibilities) who at a dinner with him, his sister, and a young male friend "at least half an angel" (Dotson Rader, according to Jo) began "to show her bitch-colors." With relish, Tennessee describes how he and the young man make fun of her and how he tells her off when she objects. He ends: "Alas, she has no Irish humor. . . . Of course, when the evening was over, I began to feel a bit sorry for Nameless. She is so tough in her loneliness, her spinsterhood, and her archaic 'principles,' which are as hypocritical as 'principles' of her vintage could possibly be."*

* Jo Healy didn't read the *Memoirs*, but a "friend" showed her the passage. Afterward, she wrote me: "This sadness has been the only situation in my entire life when I have felt so shamed and defiled that I have been unable to discuss it with any member of my family

When Sandy read the *Memoirs*, which he subtitled *Buttering Up and Knocking Down*, he decided that the Tennessee I thought I had known and liked must have been a figment of my imagination. Tennessee must always have been as unpleasant as he appeared in his book. I knew differently, and when Sandy was not convinced I searched out and gave him to read the letters Tennessee had written me over the years. They were in Xerox copies; I had put the originals in a safe-deposit box, for they had been stuffed any which way into a manila envelope as they were received and were in fragile condition. After Sandy read the Xeroxes, he said I was right: the person in the letters was as pleasant as the person in the *Memoirs* was unpleasant.

But I balked when he suggested that I write and ask Tennessee's permission for us to publish a small edition of his letters, like the one we had published earlier that year (with the permission of the Provost and Scholars of King's College, Cambridge) of E. M. Forster's letters to me. I didn't feel safe enough, or calm enough, in my relations with Tennessee to want to renege on my ten-year-old resolution not to become involved with him again.

Still, I valued our lost friendship. The end it had come to had not made it any less real or less happy in memory. And I was ashamed that I didn't trust Tennessee's assertion in the *Memoirs* that he regretted the lack of the old affection between us.* I said that if Sandy wanted to approach Tennessee with the project, and if Tennessee was willing to assign me the copyright of the letters, which I doubted, I would go along with it. Shortly before Christmas he sent off a letter. Early in January Tennessee telephoned. He said he thought the idea was good. The next week he came by our apartment with a friend, read through a small part of the Xeroxes and announced that he saw no reason why we shouldn't go ahead. His disarming agreeableness, more

---

or close friends including . . . , who has been my closest friend for most of my life. There were so many nights in the dark of my bedroom when I would blush and the agony of those remembrances is still with me."
*"Donald Windham, my collaborator on *You Touched Me*, and an early friend in New York, whose present disaffection I much regret." (Photo caption in *Memoirs*.) Later, I looked up *disaffection* in Webster's: *want of good will, esp. toward government or those in authority, disloyalty.*

like the agreeableness of the person in the letters than of the person in the *Memoirs,* did not reassure me. I asked Sandy to write a letter underlining, so there would be no misunderstanding, just what it was we were asking Tennessee for. He wrote:

6 January 1976

"Dear Tennessee:

"I'm not sure I made it clear last night *why* there should be a document giving Don the copyright to your letters to him. First of all, I would like to print the book as handsomely as possible, as I did with the Forster, which is expensive, and to sell it, as I did with the Forster, at a price to cover the expenses without losing money. Second, Don intends working hard to introduce and connect the letters (as he did with the Forster) and to make an important book from them. But he doesn't want to begin work without owning the rights. I think you can understand that, dealing as you must have to do so much with agents and lawyers and businessmen. Of course, this is an extraordinary and not a routine request that we are making of you, and the alternative is to just let the letters lie in the safe-deposit box until we are all gone. Eventually, I suppose, they would be published. But they are beautiful—in letters as beautiful as the most beautiful of your plays—and no one could edit them better than Don (who understands you as you were in the 1940s and '50s and would be friendly and not pedantic). So why should we not all have the joy of seeing them printed, and Don whatever money there might be from the book in the future? I've drafted a document which is probably not sufficiently legal but incorporates what I think should be in it. Your lawyer will know."

After Tennessee received the letter, he invited us to lunch and asked us to bring the Xeroxes so he could finish reading them. He came to supper at our apartment to return them. While he was there he signed the draft agreement Sandy had included with his letter, insisting that his lawyer needn't be involved. The agreement stated that the assignment of the copyright to me was in exchange for the sum of one dollar. Tennessee's secretary-companion, who signed as witness for him, asked for the dollar before he wrote his name.

A few days later from San Francisco, Tennessee sent a postcard:

"Dear Friends Again: The loveliest thing that can occur in the Bicentennial year is our renewed contact—I needed it so badly—and the letters to bind it all back together."

Sandy's earlier publications had been in editions of 300 copies or less. This book was to be larger, more handsome, and more expensive to print than the Forster. Before completion, his monetary investment (aside from our 700 hours of work) was $15,000. He could only hope to break even if he printed 500 copies and sold out the entire edition at $50 a copy retail. The chances of his doing this were slim. Nevertheless, we were happy. When the finished books arrived at the end of September from Italy, we were proud to show them to Tennessee. He came by our apartment the next day, on his way to be photographed endorsing Sheaffer pens, picked up copies for himself and signed twenty-six special copies on blue Fabriano paper.

As depressed as I had been that Tennessee had written the *Memoirs,* as reluctant as I had been to become involved with him again, I was glad both had happened. The publication of the *Memoirs,* by making public every area of Tennessee's privacy that his correspondence with me invaded, had made the publication of the *Letters* feasible. Despite my distrust, it seemed possible that our book *might* make us, not "Friends Again," as Tennessee said, but at least able to encounter each other in an ambience where the past retained its value.

I see that, after all, I must say something about my early friendship with Tennessee. To leave it at the statement that he was the one person I loved to whom I didn't have a physical attachment may bring up more questions than it answers.

Tennessee made a pass at me the day that Melton and I, newly arrived in New York, met him. However, he did not take my love of Melton and rejection of him as an offense. In the first place, he made a pass at almost everybody he met in those days. In the second, he was romantic. The three of us became friends and shared a sublet apartment in Manhattan that summer. But it was Tennessee and Melton who saw most of each other. I was working at the World's Fair in Flushing, selling Coca-Cola. My shift averaged more than sixty hours a week and our encounters took place mainly when he and Melton came to the fair and visited me at my stand.

I admired Tennessee from the beginning. The short stories he was writing in the early 1940s (not to be published until after the success of *The Glass Menagerie*) were as simple and perfect as short poems by William Blake. But more important, he did something I longed to do and didn't have the courage to. He put writing before knowing where he was going to sleep or where his next meal was coming from. And—although I didn't long to do this—before personal relations. It was paying off. The Theatre Guild was about to produce *Battle of Angels*.

Two years later, when Melton married (he was romantic, too, and thought I would live with him and his wife), it was Tennessee I turned to. Not with physical attachment. My empathy for him was so strong that the idea of going to bed with him was, literally, unthinkable. I turned to him feeling that I had no future except one of devoting myself to writing the way he did, no way to survive except the improvident and promiscuous way he survived, no one but him from whom to learn the rules of the game.

My admiration was increased rather than diminished by the fact that although *Battle of Angels* had failed and he could not get his stories or poems published, his devotion to his writing remained. He was penniless, borrowing when he could, no longer living in the comparative affluence of option money and grants. The winter we wrote *You Touched Me* we were two people in the same boat. But I still did not have the courage to face being improvident. When the small amount of money I had saved was gone, I took a job working for Lincoln Kirstein, editing *Dance Index* for $25 a week. Tennessee went south, searching for a warmer climate, where it would be easier to survive on next to nothing.

Despite our separation, my emotional identification with Tennessee was total. When there was a possibility that *You Touched Me* would be produced and he returned north, I tried to make it practical as well. I ceded to him the whole of the option money we received on the play. But the few hundred dollars didn't last him long. Penniless again, he came daily to Kirstein's office and wrote poems on the extra typewriter. We shared lunches. I was living in the apartment of a friend who disapproved of Tennessee and called him "an evil influence."* I considered Tennessee the saving influence in the soigné world around me. One by one, I fell out with the people who found his threadbare appearance and preoccupied manners unacceptable.

From the time I left home until Melton married, I had lived with him monogamously. Now Tennessee and I cruised wartime Greenwich Village and Times Square. It was the season of getting the colored lights going, of the target for tonight! The season of soldiers returning from overseas, of sailors on shore leave. Of "for the sins of the world are really only its partialities, its incompletions," words of Tennessee's that I wished I had written.

Early in 1943, when Tennessee went home to Saint Louis for a visit, more broke than ever, I began to look for a cheap apartment for the two of us to live in when he returned. Fortunately—in every way—this was not to happen. Audrey Wood obtained Tennessee a job writing for MGM. He went to California at a salary of $250 a week. And I met Sandy.

The success of *The Glass Menagerie* brought me one of the happiest times of my life; it justified my deepest beliefs. But its magnitude was almost too much for Tennessee. His complaint of the catastrophe of success is not an afterthought, as Truman's late invention that he never enjoyed his success is. Tennessee enjoyed his success, but he was afraid from the beginning of its complications and burdens. I do not believe it gave even him as much pure joy as it did me.

*Tennessee didn't forget this. He inscribed my copy of *Five Young American Poets: 1944*, *To Donnie with love from "an evil influence."*

Truman, as well as Tennessee, was publishing in 1975.
Early in the year, *Esquire* printed an excerpt from *Answered
Prayers* titled "Mojave." Before it appeared, Truman told me that
the magazine would begin the story on the cover, with nothing
except the title, his name, and the first ten lines of the text in
36-point type. This seemed one of his more unrealistic fantasies,
but it turned out to be the truth. It also turned out to be the
most interesting thing about the excerpt. The text didn't seem to
have any *raison d'être,* but it didn't shock me the way the pages
I'd read at his apartment had. Then, in the fall, at the same time
Tennessee's *Memoirs* appeared, *Esquire* printed a second excerpt,
"La Côte Basque, 1965."

This was a different story. The writing and the contents were
as unpleasant as the pages I had read at Truman's. The people
he portrayed this time, using real names jumbled with false
names, were his rich friends, including those I had always believed he was most fond of, the William Paleys (false) in a
"funny story" awash in menstrual blood, Lee Radziwill (real) in a
flattering description at the expense of her sister, Jacqueline
Kennedy, etc. Under one of the false names he told the story of a
woman who had trapped a socially prominent man into mar-
riage, then shot him when he found out years later about her
trashy past and was planning to divorce her. Her husband's
death was ruled an accident and, according to Truman, she got
away with murder. He had discussed the case with me at length
when it was in the newspapers. Now his version of the "facts"
was in print.

A few days after I read the excerpt I was at the office of a
book dealer, an admirer and collector of Williams and of Capote. In a pause of telling me how disappointed he had been in

Tennessee's *Memoirs,* he pushed a clipping across his desk toward me and asked if I'd seen it. It was a news item from the *N. Y. Post* stating that the death of the woman who had been portrayed as murdering her husband in Truman's piece had been due to a deliberate overdose of sleeping pills. Then he showed me an earlier clipping, which I hadn't seen either: the woman's obituary from the *N. Y. Times.* He had read the obituary the day after reading Truman's piece in *Esquire,* recognized the account of the shooting, etc., as being the same in both, and saved it.

Soon after this, Truman telephoned from California. He was living there with Johnny and acting in a Neil Simon movie, *Murder by Death.* He asked if I'd read his piece and what I thought of it. Knowing his sensitivity to criticism, even implied, I was cautious. What I had to say was too complicated to be blurted out over the telephone. I limited myself to "I'd like to talk to you about it when I see you." That was all Truman wanted to hear. He ended the conversation.

The people portrayed in "La Côte Basque, 1965," were, by and large, people who had been guests at Truman's Black and White Dance for five hundred people—"all my friends"—at the Plaza Hotel in 1966. This event had proved even more mesmerizing to the media than Truman's fabrications about his feats in writing *In Cold Blood.* The *N. Y. Times* devoted a full page to the "little masked ball": two articles by its leading society reporters, six photographs, and a list of the 540 invitees—"as spectacular a group as has ever been assembled for a private party in New York, an international Who's Who of notables." The party was treated by the media in general as a social, not a promotional, event; and certainly I have never seen Truman socially happier than he was that evening. Savoring his triumph, he believed the make-believe behind it. Perhaps his reading the names of all those "friends" officially listed in the newspaper the next day was the beginning of his ceasing to care about their actual friendships. In any case, when he was in New York at Christmas after the publication of "La Côte Basque, 1965" and we talked on the telephone, he said, referring to other people's reactions, "The mistake those people made was in thinking that the host who gave that party at the Plaza was the real me."

The idea that Truman thought of himself as having a "real" and an unreal self disconcerted me. In retrospect, I see that it should have given me an insight and served as a warning; but at the time I was mainly aware that he avoided encountering me and allowing me the chance to tell him what I thought about his story.

After Christmas, he disappeared into his life in California. In the spring, while he was still there, *Esquire* printed a third excerpt, "Unspoiled Monsters." It contained all the pages I had read six years before. At the beginning of summer, Truman returned east and spent a month in a sanatorium, Silver Hill, in Connecticut. Then he came to New York. He was without Johnny, who had remained in California. And, as always when I saw him in New York, without Jack. But now he was also without the animals. The last of the English bulls had apparently been abandoned to Jack's care at the time he took up with Johnny. I never saw any of the dogs or cats with him after that. Sometimes he was with a new friend, Rick, a bartender he had met in a bar near Times Square. But Johnny was on his mind; he talked of little but Johnny's misdeeds, amorphous in detail and hard to pin down, but very pervasive in his thoughts. He demanded continually, "Can you imagine that! Have you ever heard of anything so outrageous?"

Truman once said to me about his rich friends, "Of course, I know what those people say about me as soon as I leave the room; but while I'm there I can make them jump through a hoop." Among the reactions to the scandal in the pieces he had published, the prevalent opinion I heard was that his motivation had been a desire to get revenge for hurt vanity. Remembering his remark, I could see the suspicion of their contempt of him in it, and the defensive contempt in return. And certainly he must have received rebuffs when he introduced his lower-class acquaintances into the homes of his rich friends, as he had laughingly told me he had done. But the idea that revenge was Truman's motivation behind the pieces he had written and published did not strike me as adequate or consistent with what I knew of him.

First, I thought that perhaps he had begun to publish them

to please Johnny, to keep him interested. But as his rage against Johnny's intransigences went on, it seemed to me that he must be publishing them because Johnny wasn't fulfilling the function he was supposed to. Like his predecessors, as far as I could see, Johnny was supposed to take the place of the world that resisted accepting whatever Truman said as the truth; he was supposed to believe Truman more than Truman believed himself. Now he was refusing to play his part. He had plans of his own to take advantage of his position. Therefore, Truman decided to force the recalcitrant fragment of the world to do his will instead. He would make *tout le monde* acclaim him as the new Proust, on the basis of these demonstrations of his inability to work as he used to. With buzzard boldness, he determined to make them do it despite the fact that he was assaulting rather than seducing them, no longer using his "ability to beguile and please."* Perhaps, like Tennessee, he had come to believe that he was defending himself, not attacking others, a belief that condones all emotional and physical violence toward others with no conscious reaction except relief that one has oneself escaped harm. In any case, he had decided that he would make them swallow, not sugar-coated pills, but toads. It was as though he had subconsciously said to himself: Since no one else will collapse my house of cards, I will see if I can do it myself. As though he consciously determined to give a final test to the powers he had been led to believe in, to learn whether or not reality could be kayoed.

In December 1976, *Esquire* printed a fourth excerpt. This one, "Kate McCloud," contained a portrait, under his real name, of Montgomery Clift. Despite the identification, there is no veracity in the incident depicted. Monty is presented as a hand-trembling, space-staring drunk at the time I was seeing him most often, when *Red River* was released in 1948. This was several years before his alcoholic behavior began in the 1950s. He and Tallulah Bankhead are portrayed as meeting at a dinner party with no predisposed attitudes toward each other, although they had acted together in *The Skin of Our Teeth* in 1942 and

Music for Chameleons.

---

heartily disliked each other. The crassness of the other guests' remarks about Monty's sexual tastes, in order to drag in the hackneyed tag line of an old Tallulah story, the hatred of reality displayed, are, if possible, even more unpleasant than the portrait of Tennessee.

As had happened with the portrait of Tennessee, Truman's portrait of Monty was not mentioned between us. When I saw him, I discarded my feelings about the pieces that had appeared in *Esquire,* just as I had discarded the magazines. It was Truman as a person, not as a writer, that I was attached to. When I was in his presence, what I retained from his published portraits of Tennessee and Monty, of the society wife who had committed suicide, etc., were not their offenses to others, but their weights on his conscience, the burdens they added to the guilt he was suffering from what he had pulled off with *In Cold Blood.* This was not difficult to do. It was his misery, not the misery of others, that was before my eyes when I saw him.

The only thing besides Johnny and the adverse reactions to the pieces in *Esquire* that Truman talked about at this time was the million-dollar libel suit Gore Vidal had filed against him the fall before for remarks he had made about Gore in "An Outrageous Interview with Truman Capote," written by Richard Zoerink for *Playgirl.* Truman was gathering affidavits for his defense. According to him, Gore didn't have a Chinaman's chance of winning. As to Gore:

From my journal: "September 18, 1976. Ran into Gore yesterday as I was going out the back entrance of Rizzoli's and he was entering. He had just finished two days of giving his pretrial depositions in his libel suit against Truman. According to him, Truman doesn't have a Chinaman's chance of winning. I volunteered that our book of Tennessee's letters would be out soon. He volunteered that he had just heard from Tennessee, 'who never calls me unless he wants something.' Tennessee wanted him to drop Richard Zoerink from his libel suit, because 'he doesn't have any money,' and to sue only Truman."

The pressures on Truman had their effect. Several weeks after my encounter with Gore, Truman spent twenty-four hours at our apartment, drinking without stopping. He telephoned on

Saturday afternoon; something important had happened; could he come by right away. As soon as he arrived, he went to the kitchen where he knew the liquor was kept in a cabinet beneath the sink, mixed frozen orange juice from the refrigerator, and made himself a tumbler of orange juice and vodka. Then he came into the living room and began his account of what had happened. It was not, as I expected, something about Gore's suit. It was the same story as the last two years: Johnny had done something outrageous. Today it is as impossible for me to separate these stories as it is for me to separate Johnny's predecessors. Truman's exasperation was always disproportionate to what he presented as its cause; the details changed as quickly as his versions of where Johnny was in California: in a house Truman was renting, in a house Truman had bought, in the house of a friend of Truman's, in the house of an enemy. Whatever the story was that day, I listened; I assured him he was right; Johnny was impossible; he should have no more to do with him. Truman was silent, thought a while, then said, "Yes, but can you imagine!" and began again.

I tried to make him eat. When food was on the table, he started his litany of "one more drink." It was after midnight when I ceased trying to make him stop drinking and, if he wouldn't eat, go to bed. He refused. He spent the night on the living-room couch, dozing and sipping. When I made breakfast, he drank more orange juice and vodka, or perhaps he had finished the vodka and was on to the gin by then. Sunday evening, Sandy returned from the weekend with his mother in New Jersey. The perfidy of Johnny was expounded once more from the beginning. "Have you ever heard of anything so outrageous?" When we tried to make him eat supper, he refused and left.

In my experiences with Truman at this time, he was never deliberately cruel; but, as with Monty, after a certain point each encounter with him made anyone who was fond of him suffer.

"December 15. Yesterday, Truman was here a little after five P.M., in a terrible state. He had had lunch with his editor at Random House and spent the afternoon with his analyst, who had, according to Truman, told him he was sure Truman was going to commit suicide and had expected to hear of his death daily for the last months. Anyway, Truman was still drinking, in despair, absolutely not knowing which way to turn, weeping that no one else could help him and that he couldn't help himself. The one time he seemed to get a little outside his desperation was when I said to him that I knew things were very, very bad and he replied, 'They're worse than that!' But mostly it was like a stuck needle on a record of despair, without even the touch of perspective in that reply. He finally consented to go home, where Jack was waiting for him, when we begged him not to have another drink, which brought automatic, but brief, anger and threats ('Maybe you'll never see me again!'), and he left like a desperate child, Sandy going downstairs with him to get a taxi. I was afraid he might go somewhere else, but when I called his apartment half an hour later he was there. According to him, the analyst told him what I have said all along, that he is using Johnny to conceal from himself his real problems. Truman didn't really tell us what the analyst had said. But he himself did say at various times, 'I'm ill; I'm desperately ill and it's mental.' And 'I guess I really began to go crazy about seven years ago.'

"When I telephoned Liz Smith, to thank her for having sent me copies of her columns about the *Letters* at Truman's request, and said that he was having a hard time, she replied, 'As has happened to all of us, he's suffering from narcissistic mortification.' But I don't know what she was referring to, or what she knows about what he's going through. She might mean nothing more than his 'losing' Johnny, or his drunken fall in his bedroom a few weeks ago that broke his teeth. This tooth accident, incidentally, grimly reminds me of Monty."

"January 1, 1977. The New Year started at 2 A.M. with Jack calling to ask if Truman, who had called him earlier and said he was with me, was here. As I told him, I hadn't seen Truman or heard from him since I visited him at Roosevelt Hospital a day or two after Christmas. So I guess he is drinking again, just a day out of the hospital. At 8 A.M. Jack called to say Truman had returned some time between his first call and then and was asleep."

"January 5. Yesterday Truman came by in the late afternoon, drank what vodka was left in the bottle after I'd hidden most of it at Jack's suggestion, asked, in his first evincing of interest, how the *Letters* is selling, and bought a copy to take with him when he left."

"January 16. Truman called yesterday and asked us to lunch at the Plaza where, in contrast to the staff's past bowing and scraping, the headwaiter was cold to the point of rudeness, refused to give him the table he asked for, etc. After lunch he came here to nap, then went to see Rick, then returned already in the next-to-last state of his drinking, wanting to join the dinner party we were giving for Lois, Sanna, the B.'s, and talked nonstop all evening, never listening. When he finally left with the guests (the B.'s offering to drive everyone home), he led them to the Cowboy, a gay bar somewhere near his house, where they left him at 2 A.M. His stamina is unbelievable, leaving Sandy and me exhausted, but he is on a collision course. His conversation is total fantasy and total indiscretion: telling Sanna (a former *Harper's Bazaar* fashion editor) that he had his face lifted two weeks ago when he was in the Roosevelt Hospital (drying out), and that she should do the same, because she has good bone structure and that then she'll be a good-looking woman. Telling me Simon & Schuster has bought the commercial rights to the *Letters* (which they rejected last week), reciting to me *Time* magazine's (promised but unwritten) review of the book, announcing his three-million-dollar advance from New American Library, going on and on about his mother's suicide, his terrible love affairs, etc. The other guests, pop-eyed, take turns listening; but if everyone is exhausted at once he protests, 'You're not listening to me!' The fearful note behind all this is that Jack has gone (last Wednesday) to Switzerland and Truman is in the United Nations apartment alone."

"January 30. By Truman's apartment yesterday afternoon to see him before he left for Switzerland. The luggage was already in the living room. He was going through his various suit and overcoat pockets, his carry-on bag, storing miniatures of vodka for the trip, never mentioning it, as though his actions were invisible. He said he is suing Tennessee for five million dollars for Tennessee's statement in an interview that someone else is writing *Answered Prayers*. (When I returned home I read the clipping from the *N.Y. Post* with Tennessee's remarks. I don't think a libel suit is possible; but I hope that, at least, the rumor of it reaches Mr. Williams, for a little tit for tat.)"

· 12 ·

The copies of *Tennessee Williams' Letters to Donald Windham, 1940–1965* had arrived from the printer in Italy only a few days before I learned why Tennessee had been so casually agreeable to its publication.

The week after the copies arrived, Tennessee's agent telephoned and asked if we had a written permission from Tennessee to publish the letters; if so, to send him a copy. A week later Tennessee's lawyer telephoned and asked for the name of our lawyer so she could discuss with him what was to be done about our having published Tennessee's letters. Sandy replied that he didn't have a lawyer and asked for a written statement of her complaints before he retained one.

The letter from Tennessee's lawyer was addressed to me. It said that in response to my "flagrant" and "egregious" breaches of our agreement, Tennessee would have resort to the courts for appropriate legal remedies, including, but not limited to, action to restrain distribution of the book as well as for damages—on the grounds that without his written permission to do so I had added to the letters a foreword, an appendix, footnotes, introductory material to chapters, and corrected mistakes in typing and spelling—*unless* distribution of the limited edition was ceased "forthwith" and any copyrights relating to the book were "immediately" assigned to Mr. Williams.

While editing the book, Sandy and I had consulted Alan Schwartz, at Greenbaum, Wolff & Ernst, for advice to protect Tennessee and ourselves against possible suits for libel. Schwartz was Truman's lawyer, and had once been Tennessee's lawyer, but I had been recommended to him by a literary agent. Now we went to him for advice as to what we should do about the communication from Tennessee's lawyer.

Even before I received the letter from his lawyer, Tennessee had begun his public campaign against us. The middle of October, Liz Smith dedicated six paragraphs of her gossip column in the *N. Y. Daily News* to his outrage at the "gorgeous tome" of his private letters, which we had published to "ruin" him, and his plans for legal action to suppress it. I began to receive communications from people who hadn't read the book and wouldn't read a book in which I had presented an old friend in a bad light, and from people who had read the book and were delighted I had presented Tennessee so sympathetically that, in appreciation, he was pretending to be outraged in order to get publicity and help us sell it.

Early in December, Truman, who read the *Daily News* and knew that I didn't, telephoned that there had been a second column about the book. The call came in the middle of his shuttling in and out of hospitals. He couldn't find the item or remember the day it had appeared, and in the absence of anyone else's having mentioned it I wondered if it existed. But the next day he invited Sandy and me to lunch at Antolotti's, a restaurant near United Nations Plaza where he was now welcomed as he had once been at the Plaza, Colony, etc.;* we went by the *Daily News* offices to look through the issues for the previous week, and there the item was.

Greenbaum, Wolff & Ernst replied to Tennessee's lawyer that his agreement with me contained no conditions or restrictions, other than a direction which had been complied with to cut a racist remark, and that although Tennessee may not have consented to the publication of introductory material, etc., this was irrelevant as he had no rights in such material and no right to object.

However, Alan Schwartz warned me that although Tennessee had no case against me, certainly no case that would stand up in court, if he entered a suit as he threatened the pretrial expenses could easily cost me $15,000, and perhaps much more. This gave me pause, but I preferred to fight Tennessee rather than to act as though I were guilty of his charges. I determined that if it

---

*One night, we were with Truman at Quo Vadis. Society acquaintances of his were seated at the next table and saw him. They asked to be moved to the other room.

became necessary I would sell the original manuscripts of *Battle of Angels, Stairs to the Roof* and *A Streetcar Named Desire*, which Tennessee had given me at the beginning of his career, when their value was largely sentimental, and which I still owned.

Gerald Clarke of *Time* had bought a copy of the *Letters* for research on the biography he was writing of Truman. He planned to review the book for the magazine if the editors would allow him; after Tennessee read his review, he assured me, Tennessee would have no more objections to the book's publication. Like the general public, he believed Tennessee's pretense that the contents of the book upset him. As I foresaw, after Clarke's laudatory review appeared at the end of January, Tennessee's determination to obtain the monetary rights to the book intensified.

The interest in the *Letters* intensified, also. Commercial publishers began to approach us about a trade edition. Replying to these approaches was tricky; anyone who was interested had to be presented with Tennessee's claims against me and my defense. I put the whole business into Alan Schwartz's hands. The offer we accepted was from the CBS complex, Holt, Rinehart & Winston and Popular Library, because Holt agreed to bring out a hardback trade edition of my novel *Tanaquil* and Popular Library paperback editions of *The Hero Continues, Two People* and *Tanaquil,* as well as of the *Letters.*

From my journal: "February 26, 1977. To United Nations Plaza to see Truman who has returned from Switzerland and from several days in the hospital where he had, according to him, a throat tumor removed and his face lifted, but I suspect only the latter. He was wearing a scarf tied around his head, a knit cap pulled down over it, and a kaftan with the hood up over the scarf and cap, and dark glasses, the temples over the kaftan. 'I can't go out of the house for at least a week,' he had said on the phone, asking me to bring him some light bulbs, but when we arrived he was already out in the 22nd floor hall, hoping someone would glimpse his outfit. Happily, he wasn't drinking.

"The night before, Alan Schwartz and Gerald Clarke had been to see him and he knew all about Holt and Popular Library. 'It restores my faith enough to make me want to stay alive a couple of years more,' he was sweet enough to say."

"March 1. Truman phoned and asked, 'What's my telephone number?'"

·13·

After the *Time* review appeared, Tennessee's version of Sandy's and my perfidy changed; his claim that the *Letters* would ruin him became a claim that we had hoodwinked him and stolen the copyright.

One day I ran into Gore Vidal on Central Park South. He brought up the *Letters* and we talked for ten minutes. He had seen Tennessee in California, at Isherwood's, and Tennessee had told him we had gotten him drunk and tricked him into signing away his copyright. Gore also said that Tennessee wasn't denouncing the book but was saying, "I don't know why they've turned against me," and added: "Anyway, the glorious bird thinks the letters are valuable now and he wants the rights back."

Concerning Tennessee's remarks about him in the letters, he said: "I suppose it's all actionable. At least they show he used to be able to write. But they also show that he had a murderous streak in him as far back as the forties, to act as he did toward me and to write about me in that way." The conversation was friendly; I didn't detect any hidden hostility, despite the word "actionable."*

Gore's suit against Truman was in limbo. Truman's suit against Tennessee remained what it was, just talk. But Truman's condition, notwithstanding his cheerfulness on his return from Switzerland, was not improved.

From my journal: "March 11, 1977. To lunch with Truman, who phoned sounding depressed, saying he was upset and

---

*I was wrong. In *Views from a Window* (1980), a collection of Vidal's interviews, he goes out of his way to do me in, together with Capote, Fitzgerald, Faulkner, Hemingway, Mailer, Melville, etc., etc., etc.

wanting company. He was talking about how much money he has and the average sum people leave at their deaths, how Jack has enough to live on. And, of course, how he is through with Johnny."

Before the end of the month I went several times to visit Truman in the Regent, a depressing private hospital in the East Sixties, the elevators locked, the rooms drab and dark, the maze of halls wandered by alcoholics looking for a way of escape, asking visitors for change to make a phone call. He went directly from there to a party given by Irving Lazar at the Tavern on the Green for the Academy Awards.

After Tennessee learned of the proposed sale of the trade rights of the *Letters,* he carried his accusations of my dishonesty to the publishing world. The contracts with Holt and Popular Library still had not been signed in June, when there was a new delay. Tennessee cabled Holt from England advising them to drop their proposed publication: "Windham's acquisition of copyright was obtained under highly questionable circumstances and original publication involved total disregard of understanding between us."

Popular Library, frightened off, dropped their bid for the paperback rights.* Holt decided to go ahead with the hardback edition. In the face of this, Tennessee's agent went to their offices. He warned them that Tennessee was planning "to spend every cent he has" suing to prove his agreement with me invalid, but that he might drop his objections if a contract was drawn up dividing the royalties between him and me; and he suggested the percentages. Holt wanted me to agree, but after having been branded a criminal by Tennessee and his associates for six months, I refused to enter a business deal with them. The contract was signed with a new indemnification clause in which I assumed one-hundred percent liability for expenses incurred by any suit brought against the book by Tennessee.

I visited Truman at the Regent Hospital again in May. In

---

*Popular Library signed a contract and paid an advance for *The Hero Continues,* then did not publish it. When I asked if publication was dropped because Tennessee had threatened to sue them about this book, too, I was told it was dropped because the cover their designer made for the book was not good "packaging."

June or July he went to California to join Johnny. By September he was in New York and I was visiting him at the Regent Hospital again. Out briefly, he telephoned one Sunday from his apartment, where he was alone, asking me to bring him some soup because he had nothing to eat and—when I said I would be over as soon as I could—some vodka. He returned at the end of the month to California. Jack telephoned me from Long Island, said Truman was drinking and wanted to come back but wasn't able to alone; did I know anyone in California who could help? Mid-October he was brought to New York and entered Smithers Alcoholic Rehabilitation Center.

· 14 ·

The review of the *Letters* by Robert Brustein in the Sunday *N. Y. Times Book Review,* November 20, 1977, was a devastating denunciation of Tennessee. It read like one of his nightmares come true; yet even while reading it I remembered that a denunciation was what Tennessee had acted as though Clarke's laudatory review in *Time* had been.* Whatever Tennessee's reaction was to be, mine was to write a letter to the *Times* pointing out Brustein's distorting misstatements and defending Tennessee.

While doing it, I noted in my journal: "Tennessee's reaction will probably be an attack on me. Then I'll write: 'Nothing ever changes. Having defended Tennessee against others, now I must defend myself against him.'"

This happened. Toward the middle of December, I received a telephone call from an editor at the *Times Book Review.* He acknowledged my letter and said the newspaper wanted to send me a letter from Tennessee to answer. It was the third or fourth version they had received, following a telegram. Their lawyers had told them the letter was libelous of me and the *Book Review* could not print it unless I agreed and answered it. This seemed the best thing to do. If Tennessee was taking his lies about me from the gossip columns, the literary and the publishing worlds, to the news press, it would be best to get my answers into print.

But how had the *Times'* lawyers known his statements were lies and therefore libelous? They could hardly be as aware of the facts as I was. I learned the answer after I had sent the *Times* my reply; then they gave me copies of the earlier and overlapping

*"Williams ranks as one of the best (and least known) American letter writers . . . Through this newly discovered treasure of prose, the reader too sees and cares how it is and how it has been with America's greatest living playwright." *Time,* February 7, 1977.

letters, which not only accused Sandy and me of entirely different scenarios of villainous acts, like progressive drafts of a play written to work out what plot appeared most heinous, but were mutually contradictory. In the first he is asked to sign "some slips of paper" with typed wording "too convoluted for my understanding." In the second he is not allowed to read what is on the slips but "assured that they merely signify approval of a small Verona edition." In a third he is made too drunk to read, in a fourth he doesn't have his glasses, and in the final both of these. In each, our dealings with him, which spanned three weeks (he signed a second agreement, drawn up for me by a lawyer, on his return from San Francisco), are reduced to one impromptu evening. I was confident in answering his inventions. Still, he took me in. I believed that the *Letters* was the cause of the hostility expressed by Brustein, whom Tennessee buttered up to in his letter to the *Times* as "the dean of our country's most renowned school of drama," and I answered as though this were true. I did not discover until later that their mutual hatred, whenever it began, predated Brustein's review by at least a year. In October 1976, in an interview that was to be published early the next summer in *Gay Sunshine,* Tennessee said: "Brustein is ruthless. I don't feel temperately about this man. I'm too old to be afraid of him. Despicable! He is despicable beneath contempt."

As winter arrived, my encounters with Truman echoed those of the winter before.

From my journal: "November 23, 1977. Had lunch yesterday with Truman at Antolotti's. 'Have a drink,' he said. I refused. He had a double Stolichnaya with orange juice on the side. (Only that one for a miracle.) Two weeks ago, on the way home from his cure at Smithers, he jumped out of the taxi, leaving Jack, 'to go to a movie.' A day later, he came by our apartment, having just seen a porno movie alone; although he didn't ask for a drink I could see that his whole being was concentrated on deciding how to, whether or not to, and after talking compulsively about Johnny, he lapsed into a blankness in which he didn't even reply to questions. That was Thursday.

Sunday he was drunk at the reading he was to give in Baltimore and led off the stage. He was in Doctors Hospital Wednesday through Saturday. 'I'll just have to live on Antibuse,' he said on the phone. Then I saw him for the first time yesterday, Tuesday. After the drink and a bowl of soup, he was inaudible and not listening, but at least he said he wanted to leave and go take a nap. Not at home, however, he said when we were on the street, at the gym. I walked him there and left him at the door. When I arrived home in about an hour, I telephoned the United Nations apartment to tell Jack where I'd left him, but Truman answered. 'The gym was noisy,' he said."

Despite Truman's state, he continued to be interested in my difficulties with Tennessee and partisan in his attitude.

"January 2, 1978. Still fighting my cold. But the top story to start the New Year: Truman called to tell me Alan Schwartz had been to see him (vague as to when, in the last few days) and said both M . . . and Tennessee had telephoned him to ask him to be Tennessee's lawyer in a suit *against me* and that they had replied, when told that it was impossible because he is my lawyer, 'Well, these things can be arranged.' As good as I am at foreseeing Tennessee's moves, this one takes me by surprise."

Besides coming down with a cold, I had fallen into a depression. As the mid-January publication of the exchange of letters in the *Times* approached, the cold was joined by diarrhea, vomiting, etc. I recovered enough to fly to the Bahamas with Sandy before the fifteenth. Truman had gone with friends to Martinique. He sent us a postcard; it said he had enjoyed my precise letters in the *Times* and that the general opinion of the people with him was that Tennessee was a fool.

In March, on Alan Schwartz's recommendation that it would help Truman, I talked to a West Coast journalist, Anne Fleming, who was writing an article on Truman for the *N. Y. Times Magazine*. Truman, when he learned that I had eaten lunch with her, was cross. "She's interviewing everybody and she hasn't even *spoken* to me," he complained. Sandy and I were having dinner with him and Rick before going to a party for five hundred people Truman and Andy Warhol were hosting for Kodak at Studio 54. Over dessert, he mentioned that Dotson Rader, a "friend" of his and of Tennessee's, was writing an article on the *Letters* for *London Magazine*. Asked by Sandy if the article was to be hostile to me, Truman clammed up. "That's all I know. He only mentioned it on the telephone. He's writing an article. Period."

That evening also put a period to my hearing about Johnny. Studio 54, with its air of mobbism and snobbism, its flashing lights and blasting sound, jammed with the guests invited to this party where the liquor flowed gratis from the bar and the trays of the nearly naked waiters, was the most infernal of the few times I went there with Truman. In the alcoholic dark, people I didn't know were talking to me face to face. "That man behind you eavesdropping on what you're saying is Tennessee Williams' agent," a stranger in a business suit whispered in my ear. Another, looking like a race-track tout, who had watched me talking with Truman, confided, "Truman won't be bothered by Johnny anymore. I've scared him off by firebombing his car."

The stories I'd been hearing, from Truman and others, about Johnny, had become increasingly melodramatic in the last months—stolen cash, stolen handguns, stolen automobiles—and for that reason increasingly memorable, if not increasingly believable. This seemed the most unbelievable of all; but, fact or fiction, it was the last word I heard about Johnny. Truman never mentioned this compulsive subject to me again.

"April 21. Truman, on the Dick Cavett show, says that he hasn't and has never had a drinking problem, tells the story about Garbo wanting to do *Dorian Gray* from Tennessee's letters to me, as though it is something she told him, says his father was married seven times, etc. Better appearance, despite some twitches, than I expected. But what a lesson, to anyone interested, in his ability to face truth and reality."

·15·

I wanted to help Truman, but it was not always easy to know how. One Sunday toward the end of June, he called me from the Regent Hospital at eleven-thirty in the morning. He wanted me to come over at noon and have lunch with him— and to "bring him a little something," which he specified when I asked if that was what he meant, was "to drink." I refused. "That's not what I'm here for," he protested; "I'm just so nervous I have to have something to calm me down." I repeated my refusal; I had to make my own decision about that. Sounding desperate, he said that in that case he would just have to find some way to get out of there for a while, but why didn't I come over at twelve-thirty? I decided not to go. The telephone rang at twelve and again at twelve-thirty. I didn't answer, fearing it would be Truman repeating his urging for me to bring him something to drink. But I couldn't leave it at that if he was calling and hoping to see me, so at one o'clock I went over. He seemed calm and resigned, not at all desperate, when I arrived. He didn't mention his request, or even seem as though he were avoiding doing it. There was a lunch tray for me, which I re- fused. He ate the cherry cobbler. His jar of milk was refilled. Except for his seeming drowsy at times, it was a pleasant, com- municative visit. Halfway through, he persuaded the nurse to give him an injection of something. He said that the *N. Y. Times* had brought Anne Fleming back to New York and that her arti- cle on him was coming out in two weeks, on July 9. The people he had talked to at the *Times* had assured him that it was sympa- thetic.

"But," he added with an old-time laugh, "that depends on who's reading it."

Shortly before the appearance of the article, which had been divided into two installments, Anne Fleming telephoned from California. She was looking for more photographs to illustrate the second part. I lent the *Times* a postcard of me, Truman, his mother and Joe Capote that had been taken in Piazza San Marco when we were in Venice in the fall of 1950.

When I read the first of the two installments I admired parts of it, although I didn't see how it could help Truman and couldn't guess how he would take it. The photograph of him on the cover, which I remembered he had told me he approved of, struck me as the most unpleasant thing. Before I talked to Truman, I spoke to Alan Schwartz. He said Truman was upset by the article's lack of sophistication about his work and by its "gossip"; the only thing Truman liked was the cover photograph.

On Friday of the next week I received the second part of the article, sent me by the *Times* with the photograph I had lent them. The two parts did not add up to as much as I had hoped they would; the amount of private information revealed didn't seem justified by an equal amount of understanding. I was depressed, especially as Sandy and I came out as his two most-mentioned friends and one of Anne Fleming's main sources of information. On Saturday when I talked to Truman, who had just read the installment, I didn't tell him I had seen it.

He was very bright, not yet sure, as far as I could tell, what his final attitude was to the quotes from Sandy and me, which included the stories of his showing Oliver's house as his own, his appropriation of Sandy's first sight of Brando, etc., all lacking in print the affection with which they had been told. He did not mention them, but about the article he said several times, "After all, it doesn't matter." And, "*You* come out very well in the photograph in Venice," clearly meaning that he, his mother and stepfather didn't. He gave the impression of putting a brave face on I-wasn't-sure-just-what situation; but perhaps on his being displeased that other people were too much in the article even more than on his being displeased at many of the reflections on him; but still pleased enough. It was *his* article. One way or another, sooner or later, he would turn it to his advantage and come out on top. He ended by saying he was in town for the weekend and we'd do something together.

"Monday, July 17. Spent from noon until nearly four yester-day having lunch with Truman. I don't really want to write it down, but I suppose I should. We met at St. John's, nearer to a neighborhood bar than a restaurant. He had three Stolichnayas straight off. The effect wasn't the worst I've seen but bad enough. Sandy's remark about him and Monty and Tennessee now being three of a kind in their misery rankles in his mind, but it was at the beginning, good-humoredly, that he mentioned it. At his drunkest, his words slurring monotonously, his mouth full of the hamburger he finally ordered, he said that his real trouble, deep down beneath everything else, is that he doesn't want to write anymore, not that he has what's called a writer's block, but that he doesn't want to be a writer anymore. Telling me not to tell anyone, even Sandy, he said Tennessee had phoned Alan and warned him not to let Sandy print Truman's letters to me. Weeping, he made incoherent statements about Mrs. Paley (who died ten days ago). He told me almost unend-ing fantasies of whom he's recently had sex with (South Amer-ican diplomats with their wives watching, Mrs. Fleming's husband, etc.) and of the offer of a $50,000 a night lecture tour for him and Norman Mailer, eight weeks, five nights a week, which he began by saying Alan was urging him to do and ended, after my protest against the idea, that Alan too was against it. 'Of course,' he said, 'I'd have to spend a few days in the hospital first.'

"After the hamburger, when he had largely regained his co-herence and I said, at three o'clock, that it was time we should go, he insisted on having another vodka. 'If I go home now I'll be sick. You can't abandon me.' This way, he added, he could take a nap when he got home and then Bob (another 1970s friend) would be there. 'I know I'm going to lose Bob' was his muttered refrain at one point.

"A manager from Peartree's, across the street, came early on, trying to lure Truman over for a drink, saying the bartenders and the customers were in tears because he wasn't there. When we came out of St. John's at twenty of four, and I was hoping to get Truman home, we met the manager again (Truman intro-ducing me to him as 'one of the five best living writers in the world today'), and I left Truman going off with him for another drink.

"But my heart isn't in writing this down and it hardly touches the hopelessness of what went on.

"At one point, trying to sell me on the sexual attractiveness of someone he said was making tents for his next party and I asked a question that he misunderstood, he asked: 'Don't you know about my new party? Haven't you read today's Sunday *Times*? It tells all about it!' And even at his clearest he was simply proud of all the quotations from him in the article.

"When we first entered St. John's he did his little sashaying TV entrance dance and said to the bartender and waitresses, 'Well, did you get your kicks reading today's N. Y. *Times Magazine* section?'"

"July 18. At breakfast I see in the paper that Truman is on the Stanley Siegel show at 9 A.M.—and there he is, in the same shirt I left him in Sunday afternoon, saying he hasn't been to bed for 48 hours, midway drunk of the stages I saw him in, looking as though he'd fall asleep any minute, calling forth pity but also despair; one new note—he has now latched on to classifying himself with Monty and Marilyn Monroe and announced that he would probably kill himself, like them, by accident."

THREE

.

*"The armour of falsehood is subtly
wrought out of darkness, and hides a
man not only from others, but from his
own soul."*

—E. M. Forster, *A Room with
a View*

· 16 ·

As I draw near the close of these pages, I fear I am ending up, not with a delicate French nougat, but with a hard Italian torrone, a torrone to break your teeth on. In any confectionery of the heart it would be labeled "serve at your own risk." Some of my ingredients resemble almonds less than oil of bitter almond, from which only with skill can the poison be removed. Others, that I would like to discard but cannot, are downright rotten. Thus:

"Professionally, Donald Windham is known, if known at all, as a writer of effetely precious prose. He is a person of dainty sensibility who trips through life with pursed lips and the air of injured vanity. Having studied his edited version of Williams' letters one discovers that what one always suspected about him is true, namely that under the treacle prose, bitter like a spoiled cherry covered in sweet chocolate, are the petty resentments and embittered false pride rubbed sore by too little achievement in too long a career."

Among the other judgments and epithets about me that I found waiting in Dotson Rader's "The Private Letters of Tennessee Williams," when the July issue of *London Magazine* arrived, were: pernicious, lacking in decency, self-serving, self-deluded, arrogant, dishonest, humorless, touchy, whining, reprehensible, permanently derailed, jealous, a squirrel, a scavenger, a peddler, a failed writer, a false friend, around only when I needed something.

Everything in the article was fake except the hatred; that was frighteningly real; and since I didn't know Rader and he didn't know me, and he was a semipermanent houseguest of Tennessee's, the hatred could only be Tennessee's.

Not that any statement about me in the article was explicitly attributed to him. In the eleven pages of vituperation the only person cited to corroborate the main criminal accusation, that I had published the *Letters* without Tennessee's consent or knowledge, was Truman. "You won't believe it," he is quoted as saying when he tells Rader of the existence of the *Letters;* "Tennessee is going to be furious."

Truman is also credited with telling Rader an equally fictitious "funny story": its point is less that Tennessee and I were beaten up by two sailors, tied to straight chairs and left helpless for forty-eight hours in a hotel that charged us double occupancy for two days, than that the real awfulness for Tennessee was having to listen to my conversation for that long.

But most of the fabrications were implicitly Tennessee's: that he had been a "National Foundation of the Arts for Donald Windham" and supported me from the 1940s through the 1960s, during which time I never "got off my arse" and found a job, but sold his letters and manuscripts as I received them, etc. Rader (a "retired male hustler," according to the jacket of one of his books, which I sought out to learn something about this Quintus Slide journalist)* didn't have the skill to make the shower of accusations he rained on me real enough to convince anyone who knew me or had read my writing; but that only emphasized the hatred behind them.

It is a terrible thing to have blind hatred directed toward you. Its malevolent waves make you understand the power of the evil eye, of black magic, charms and spells, of pins stuck in voodoo dolls. Its effect is not lessened when accompanied by a threat of assassination, as it was in Rader's article. "One marvels at Williams' patience in not taking out a Mob contract on the whole wretched crew. [Me, Brustein and the *N. Y. Times*] Perhaps he has."

For a day and a half I managed to convince myself the article was so ludicrous I should ignore it, despite the fact that *London Magazine* is a literary publication with a distinguished past, the copies of which are bound and preserved on library shelves all over the world. Then at 3 A.M. on the second night, my mind

---

*According to Gore Vidal: "A little cunt. A real cunt." *Fag Rag* 7/8, reprinted in *Gay Sunshine Interviews,* Vol. 1.

circling too tirelessly to let me sleep, I got up and wrote out a refutation of Rader's accusations to give to Alan Schwartz and ask him to send under his name to *London Magazine*.

For a week after Truman's appearance on the Stanley Siegel show, which was stopped midway when he became incoherent, helplessly turning his head this way and that, he was in the Regent Hospital. I telephoned the day before he was to be released, not wanting to think of his returning to the United Nations Plaza apartment alone, and asked him to come stay with us on Fire Island; it wasn't necessary, he was going directly from the hospital to Hazelden, a clinic in Minnesota.

From my journal: "July 31, 1978. Her niece Erin calls to tell me Jo Healy died Friday of a heart attack. What gratuitous unhappiness Tennessee caused her the last three years of her life and how sensitive it made her to other people's unhappiness. My last call from her, a week ago, was about her concern for Truman, urging me to telephone him at the hospital, rather than wait for him to phone me, so he wouldn't feel I had abandoned him."

When I called Alan Schwartz to get Truman's address in Minnesota, he told me that he had received no phone call from Tennessee as Truman had told me that black Sunday, that Truman must have been remembering Tennessee's earlier one asking Alan to be his lawyer against me.

I was having continual nightmares. In one I was reading a book of medical advice: for a broken heart, lie down three hours; for a headache, cut off your left arm.

"August 12. A postcard from Truman at Hazelden to Sandy and me, saying: 'Having wonderful time. Wish *you* were here. No, I wouldn't wish that on my best friends, which you are.'"

When I thought he would feel up to reading it, I sent him a copy of Rader's article.

"August 26. Talked to Truman, who phoned from Minnesota to say he'd written a 'strong' letter to *London Magazine*. I wish he'd sent me a copy."

My preoccupation with Truman made me begin to see reflections of him everywhere.

"August 28. Strange parallels in the last chapter of the Raymond Chandler biography to situations of Truman's, especially in his trying, through the wives, to insert himself into families, the way Truman does through the husbands; so it isn't necessarily a homosexual situation, as one would gather from the Fleming article. Saddest of all, the similar 'but the truth is I really want to die' statements."

Truman returned from his cure after two months. My first contacts with him were not reassuring.

"October 8. Truman telephones, with a bad cold. Says he has just returned from a lecture tour of the Northwest!"

On one visit to our apartment he did something I gave little thought to at the time but that was enough out of character for me to note it:

"November 1. Truman by to see me for an hour last evening before going to dinner next door; not drinking, a little shaky, intent on examining the E. M. Forster biography."

Alan Schwartz had said I had a clear case of libel under English law; at his suggestion I wrote a more detailed refutation of Rader's article and he sent it to his London associates. During one of my conversations with him, I learned that Truman was drinking again; he had not been, as he assured me, on the wagon since July.

"November 22. Thanksgiving. Here alone, working. Spoke to Truman, who told me Tennessee had telephoned the day before to ask him to dinner with Rader."

This was the first of a series of calls in which he teased me with news of such invitations.

"December 1. Truman by (not drinking) at drink time, before going to meet Bob and his sons for dinner nearby."

This is the last time I have seen Truman. Although I didn't dream it, Tennessee's courting of him was the beginning of the end.

I didn't dream, either, at the start of 1979, that two more years would pass before I received the printed retraction I was seeking from *London Magazine*.

I did realize, however, from the time I first heard from the British solicitors, that they found my word suspect in contrast to Tennessee's as presented by Rader. Schwartz knew both our characters and all the circumstances. But why should uninformed strangers believe that someone as important as Tennessee would bother to make up such lies about someone as unimportant as me?

An early letter, requesting clarification of points I had ignored as outside the question of libel, asked: Is the story told by Capote of your and Williams' being beaten up and tied to straight chairs for forty-eight hours by two sailors "materially true"?

I could read between the lines that the depiction of my character in the article was as little doubted as Truman's most extravagant inventions to the press. The fact that I was seeking only a retraction and not a million pounds seemed to convince them I had no case. I was told at one point that the retraction I wanted could not "possibly" be printed because it would be libelous of Rader.

London Magazine had not printed the letter Truman told me he had sent them. I had checked the issues each month at the N.Y. Public Library. Nor had Truman received an acknowledgment. Deciding that his letter must have gone astray, I asked him the next time he telephoned to write another or to give Schwartz an affidavit denying that he had made the statements attributed to him. These seemed things he should be glad to do.

He had written an eloquent letter some years before to the *N. Y. Review of Books* defending Richard Avedon against a bad review (by Robert Brustein). Only a couple of years earlier Sandy had given Truman's lawyers an affidavit denying that he had heard Truman promise part of his royalties from *In Cold Blood* to the journalist from Kansas we had watched him show Oliver Smith's house to, and who had cited Sandy as a witness to this in a suit against Truman. I had heard Truman's gratefulness to the people who had given him depositions for his defense against Gore Vidal's libel suit, and listened to his vilification of Lee Radziwill, who had refused to give one corroborating that she had told him the stories he had attributed to her. Truman's response was to reply that he would ask Alan if it was necessary.

And once more he told me that Tennessee had invited him to dinner with Rader, adding, "Of course, I wouldn't go, out of loyalty to you."

I began to receive subtle pressures from England to drop my suit. First, it was pointed out that if a negotiated settlement was not reached, my presence in that country would be "unequivocally" required to pursue my claim. Then the more upsetting news was sent that, since I was resident in the United States and not within the jurisdiction of the English courts, I could be required to deposit in a British bank a sum of money (amount not even hinted at) as security to pay the defendants' expenses if I lost.

"January 14, 1979. Talked to Truman on the telephone. Told him of the news from London and urged him again, as strongly as I could, to write Alan a note saying Rader's quotations of him are untrue. Impossible to tell whether he will or not. 'Dotson doesn't have any money,' he said. Also, he told me Rader has learned about the suit and says he doesn't know what he's done for me to be picking on him."

Two months of silence from Truman followed. Just before it ended:

"March 16. Yesterday, out of nowhere, Gerald Clarke phoned (the first time since before the *N. Y. Times* articles on

Capote appeared last July). Said he was just calling to ask how I am. 'What's the point of suing Rader?' he asked. 'He doesn't have any money.' Also: 'What does Truman have to do with it?'"

I still tried to believe in Truman's friendship; I remembered his problems; but now I could not forget my own, and the weight of the effort made the crash all the heavier when it came.

"March 22. Sandy phoned Truman last night. The moment he mentioned that Truman was failing me (and himself) in the Rader matter, Truman became openly hostile; so was Sandy; and so that is that. None of my problems are important enough to Truman to be real to him; he doesn't know what we are talking about; I am not close enough to his concerns to be a feeling entity in his conscience.

"As sad as the impasse is, it is a rest, a relief. One simply cannot go on 'fighting shadows and being defeated by them' (*Bleak House*). Unfortunately, this relief resembles the state I recognize in Tennessee that leads one to having enemies because 'you can choose your enemies, but you can't choose your friends' (Graham Greene). With friendship, the choice must always be double. It's a relief to be enemies when it's too exhausting to be friends. And we all have less energy all the time."

In the April issue of Andy Warhol's *Interview* magazine, which appeared a week later, Truman, in his tape-recorded "conversations," in reply to the question: "Did you have a big falling out with Tennessee Williams?" answered: "Somewhat. But we're friends again. He was very kind to me when I was ill. We had dinner a month ago."

Talking about his lawsuits, he emphasized: "I'm not a letters-to-the-editor person. I never write letters to the editor. If I have a motto, one that represents everything, it's 'Never write a letter to the editor.'"

This had probably been recorded in February.

One Sunday evening early in April, Truman telephoned and asked Sandy if he had received the letter he had written and sent from Spain (?), enclosing a letter to Alan Ross, the editor of *London Magazine*.

"Call me when you get it," he said.

The next day's mail did not have a letter from Truman. It did have a copy of the April 1 *Sunday Miami Herald Magazine* sent by Melton from Florida, with an article in it on Tennessee. The article extensively quoted Dotson Rader and portrayed him and Richard Zoerink (who wrote the interview with Truman which brought on Gore's libel suit) both living with Tennessee in Key West. "The two young men fulfill many roles," it said, "sons, valets, chauffeurs, audience, companions."

A month passed.

Early in May, Sandy and I returned to the apartment one afternoon to find a large envelope which Truman had left with the doorman. It contained a smaller envelope with Spanish stamps and a postmark of April 2, mailed to the wrong address and returned to Truman, whether via Spain or not wasn't clear. In it were a twelve-page letter to Sandy and a four-page letter to Ross, which he asked Sandy to forward.

The letter to Sandy wanted us to apologize for our "unjustness" and to appreciate Truman's all-out effort to understand our loss of perspective. The letter to Ross was a formal repudiation of "remarks attributed to me by Mr. Rader, remarks I never made, specifically an allegation that Mr. Williams was 'furious' because Mr. Windham had published his letters without his consent or knowledge," and an equally formal defense of me: "Mr. Windham is exceedingly well regarded as a writer and, generally speaking, is well known as a man of integrity."

My journals for 1979 and 1980 are filled with details of the progress of my libel suit against *London Magazine*. My files are stuffed with correspondence about it—not twice as long as *Remembrance of Things Past*, but twice as thick as the manuscript of my longest novel. Suffice it to say: the case was settled with a statement in Open Court, in November 1980, at the Queen's Bench Division of the High Court of Justice in London. The Counsel for the Second and Third Defendants, Alan Ross and *London Magazine*, agreed that Rader's article was "highly defamatory," was "without any foundation whatever," was "wholly without justification," and agreed to pay my legal expenses. Earlier, Rader, being resident in the United States, out of the jurisdiction of the British courts, had been judged in default of appearance. As far as I know, he got off without it costing him a cent. The Feb./March 1981 issue of *London Magazine* carried, as agreed in the court settlement, a nine-page retraction of the untrue statements in Rader's eleven-page article.*

But this victory took place after the end of the story I have yet to tell.

*In the fall of 1981, Dotson Rader was identified in the *Los Angeles Times* and other newspapers as the journalist who had confirmed a gossip-column item which said that President Jimmy Carter had bugged Blair House while President-elect Ronald Reagan was resident there. This had led the *Washington Post* to publish the item. President Carter threatened to sue the *Post* for libel. The *Post*, after an investigation, printed a front-page retraction and apology.

[Addendum, 1986: In a book on Williams published in the spring of 1985, Rader repeated part of his *London Magazine* article and stated that my suit against him and the magazine had been settled out of court. Alan Schwartz once more told me that I had a clear case of libel; but, remembering the drawn out two years of my previous suit, I decided to spare myself the added job of pursuing through the American courts these fabrications that the English court had already labeled defamatory and without any foundation, justification, or substance whatever.]

· 17 ·

The lake-front terrace of the Albergo Catullo in Sirmione was shaded by a vine-covered pergola. Between the hotel and the terrace a shabby rose garden, full of spiders and lizards, lay in the sunshine. After Truman ceased to get in touch with me early in 1979, searching for some understanding among the contradictory facts I knew about him, I recalled the mornings we sat at a metal table in the rose garden, or at one of the sturdier tables beneath the pergola, and opened our mail.

Beyond us, against the backdrop of the mountains on the far side of the lake, the ping-ping of the metal rings sounded as the fishermen mended their nets on the wharf; in the orphanage next door the children murmured their prayers or clattered in wooden clogs, shouting at the top of their voices.

We talked. Almost every mail brought Truman a letter from Newton Arvin. They had been friends since the beginning of the 1940s, when Truman was at Yaddo, where Arvin was director. He was separated from his wife and she was jealous of Truman, who was pleased by this. I suspect that his friendship with Arvin was the first real affair of Truman's life. Through most of the decade, he visited for weekends at Smith College in Northampton, where Arvin was a professor of English. But their friendship was only one of the anecdotes that made up Truman's conversation in Sirmione, like one of the colors in the garden Rilke describes where "from a million tiny insuppressible movements a mosaic of most convincing life is created."

Now, thirty-one years later, seated on the deck at Fire Island, seeking understanding, I asked myself what combination of these details and those that followed could explain what had happened. What were the elements, were I able to make a book about our friendship, that would render its course explicable?

Starting with Truman's interest in Melton's loyalty to me, the detail that had brought us together, and remembering his emotional and material generosity, his fondness for Arvin and the other friends he talked about in Sirmione, his compassion for his mother and Joe Capote, how could I arrive at the present?

After recalling the pleasure Truman took in using me as a looking glass to see himself in when he bought expensive cars and paintings throughout the 1950s, I remembered a day in the summer of 1966. We were walking down Fifth Avenue. He said offhand, "I think I'll give a big party; let's go into Tiffany's and order the invitations." In we went; and at the stationery counter he wrote out with feigned casualness—so well feigned that later the engraved cards had to be added to and corrected in pen and ink—the invitation to his Black and White Dance at the Plaza Hotel. I remembered that he had sent one of them to Sandy's mother, including her, even though they had never met, among his five hundred friends. But these and the other recollections included here offered no path to lead me to the present. Then I remembered that it was also a question of loyalty which had separated us and I decided that perhaps I had started at the wrong end. Perhaps I should begin at the present and try to work my way back.

I knew that, whether or not Truman had told the stories Rader attributed to him, he was capable of telling almost any story about me or anyone else in order to be amusing or important. I knew that although Truman might have sent the first letter to *London Magazine* as he said, or might have believed he had sent it when he hadn't, he might also never have intended sending it. At the same time, I knew that he was incapable of conspiring with Rader and Tennessee against me. I saw that his reaction to Tennessee's courting of him could well have been simple pleasure at this proof that not all real people (by his standards, people whose names appeared regularly in the media) had dropped him, that he might, after all, continue to be courted as in the past. I reminded myself that, with his own situation hardly real to him, my situation could not have been real enough to have entered into his reaction. It was far easier for me to understand that Truman wanted and expected to have my and Tennessee's and Rader's simultaneous friendships, to have all three of us believe that he had knocked himself out for each of us and to receive our congratulations and thanks,* than to understand his having telephoned William Paley—as I had read he did after his pseudonymous portrait of the Paleys was published in *Esquire*—wanting and expecting Paley's thanks for his having immortalized him and his wife in *Answered Prayers*. If Truman had been crushed and bewildered when this didn't happen, how much easier to understand that he was impatient and annoyed when he didn't receive my thanks for something he felt he had done and which I, bewilderingly, couldn't see?

I told myself that Truman had betrayed not me but himself. He had possessed my friendship and he hadn't possessed Tennessee's; and as was his wont, he hadn't valued what he had, because he had it, and had valued what he didn't have, because he didn't have it.

But none of these rationalizations succeeded in leading me to the past any more than my examination of the past had succeeded in leading me to the present. I decided that perhaps my view of what had happened was a personal distortion. Perhaps, as Cyril Connolly had suggested in *Horizon*, Truman's story was the inevitable story of the American "Book Business."† Certainly the publishing world had begun with "Get Capote," had made him and smothered him with laurels. Now hatred was being vented on him from all directions. And if Truman appeared largely to have brought his fate down on himself by his own actions, perhaps it was, nevertheless, inevitable that the same element in him that had collaborated with the "Book Business" and had been used by it to exalt and exploit his salability would eventually collaborate, despite his seeming to dominate it, with that business's efforts to gain the last possible profits from his notoriety before clearing the way for his successors.

But I felt that this scenario, like the others, lacked something essential; and the reader may well feel that I have concealed something, that I have left something out. I feel it, too. But I have put down all I know. I have come to the conclusion that it

---

*That he did is indicated by three of the ten titles he listed of "Neglected Books of the Twentieth Century" in *Antaeus*, Autumn, 1979: Dotson Rader, *Government Inspected Meat*; Tennessee Williams, *Letters to Donald Windham, 1940–1965*; Donald Windham, *The Warm Country*.

†Jean Stafford's and Robert Lowell's stories are not without similarities.

is something I have retained, which needs to be eliminated, not something I have left out, which needs to be included, that causes my confusion. My failing, I fear, is my inability to distance myself, to remove my emotions from this closing section. And if I cannot remove my emotions from the end of this story, should I not, at least about it, remain silent? But that would mean also remaining silent about the beginning. What I have said earlier cannot stand without its end and I would rather leave myself wide open than draw my reminiscences to a close with a skillfully written and apocryphal scene like Truman's description of the "farewell encounter" of Gide and Cocteau in Taormina. Since I have staggered toward my conclusion, leaning this way and that on quotations, a quotation (or two) more will not hurt. "It is no worse, because I write of it. It would be no better, if I stopped my most unwilling hand. It is done. Nothing can undo it; nothing can make it otherwise than as it was."*

Faced with this reality, I understood only that I did not understand. For me, Truman had gone through the looking glass.

For example: in Anne Fleming's article on Capote, Newton Arvin has been turned into this gray stone: "a Harvard English professor, the first man he took from a wife, inviting thereby the envy of both women and men," and with whom Truman "lived for four years," a four years there is no place for in the chronology of Truman's life.

An easy enough mistake for a journalist to make, wading through the morass of contradictory scenarios. But, seated on the deck at Fire Island, with the view of the low sand dunes, beach grass and poison ivy stretching before me to the ocean, I read in Truman's "conversations" in *Interview* his description of Arvin (who taught at Smith for thirty-seven years, and for only one, as an exchange professor, at Harvard) as a "professor at Harvard who I spent a long time with."

The statement in the Fleming article that Truman objected to most vociferously was a quotation from an unnamed acquain-

---

*Charles Dickens, *David Copperfield*. Searching to check this quotation, I found, a few pages further on, one of those Dostoevskian insights that occur now and then in Dickens, describing how David's ceasing to believe in Steerforth's worthiness softened him more toward all that was good in Steerforth, made him do more justice to the best qualities in him, than at the height of his devotion. "I am not afraid to write that I never had loved Steerforth better than when the ties that bound me to him were broken." Etc.

tance that what Truman wanted to be more than anything was a beautiful woman. Anyone who knew him, he protested, knew that this was the opposite of the truth. Now he published in *Esquire* a story titled "Dazzle," telling how he nurtured a secret wish, beginning when he was six years old, which worried him from the first thing in the morning until the last thing at night and after two years made him steal a jewel from his grandmother and give it to a New Orleans laundress reputed to have the power of making dreams come true. "I don't want to be a boy," he begs her. "I want to be a girl."

Like "Dazzle," the pieces in *Interview* were "nonfiction." Writing fiction necessitates changing reality. From the other side of the looking glass, Truman's reality seemed to be not only not mine but not his. His father has had five wives, seven wives, nine wives. "I wrote most of *In Cold Blood* in Switzerland." But what about the other version? "Many people thought I was crazy to spend six years wandering around the plains of Kansas."

One day the year before, at our apartment, Truman had said "Well, even if I never finish *Answered Prayers,* it's better known than most books that are published." He had created another category: the nonwritten novel. Now he claimed that the tape-recorded pieces in *Interview* were written in a new style that expressed his "understanding of the difference between what is true and what is *really* true" by using everything he had learned about writing "from film scripts, plays, reportage, poetry, the short story, novellas, the novel."

What is *really* true. Perhaps it was sloppy transcribing, but he now said in a piece in *Vogue:* "For four years, roughly from 1968 through 1972, I spent most of my time reading and selecting, *rewriting** and indexing my own letters, other people's letters, my diaries and journals. . . ."

There used to be a TV program called *To Tell the Truth.* One of five guests, each of whom claims to be the same person but gives different answers to questions about his activities and opinions, is the person he claims to be and stands up at the end of the program. Thinking of Truman throughout the summer, searching among the simple but contradictory facts I knew

*My italics.

about him and those he claimed about himself, I realized that he could be all five of the guests—and none of them, or all of them, could be the one to stand up at the end.

The last piece I read in *Interview,* seated on the deck at Fire Island, listening to the sound of the waves, was a long sequence of Truman's night-thoughts after he had "jacked off," gone to sleep, and waked up. It included a one-hundred-plus-words verbatim quotation of a "remembered" conversation with E. M. Forster, no time, no place, in which Forster unburdened to Truman the torment his erotic desires had given him from the time he was a schoolboy until he was in his seventies.

In December, as the holiday season which we had spent together many times approached, it was a year since I had seen Truman. As I have said, we were never invited to the same places. It was in the milieu of friendship, not of Manhattan, that we encountered.

From my journal: "December 27, 1979. This afternoon the phone rang about 4 P.M. It was Truman. He said he'd just called to wish me a Merry Christmas. Throughout the call there was no hint from him, and only one from me right before the end, that he hadn't talked to me recently or that there was any estrangement between us that wasn't minimal. He asked how I was, then launched into a ten-minute description of his new illness, reinfecting sinuses, curable by only one Canadian doctor, who will arrive here to begin treating him next week at New York Hospital, of how he has been writing in a new, etc., style and finished a really good book, a 400-page book that is only 250 pages long, of how he had won his suit against *Blue Boy,** but that no one should ever sue anyone because 'my lawyer, Alan Schwartz, left Greenbaum, Wolff & Ernst and I had to pay them all at once' in his case with 'Gore and his ambulance-chaser lawyer.' He didn't ask about my libel suit, or if I'd written anything, or a word beyond how are you. I brought up at the end that I hadn't seen him for a year or spoken to him in almost that time. Then he said that when he's out of the hospital he'd like to come see us

*For printing a presumed interview with him which he said he never gave.

or us to come see him. I said for him to call and we'd see. 'If there's any iota of good to see in me I'd like it to be seen,' he said. 'Ditto,' I replied, 'What?' 'Ditto.' 'Oh, ditto. Well, goodbye.'

"He did say he'd gotten from Sandy the letter returning to him the right he'd given us to publish his letters to me, 'but I wasn't thinking about that at all.' And he said he didn't understand Sandy's earlier reply to his letter from Spain; but that only led to a very brief replay of his defense of himself and invitation for an apology, and I cut it off.

"Whatever he wanted, it did not depend on any response, any personal response, from me."

Perhaps Truman was beginning to miss me as I had missed him all summer. The void left by the end of a thirty-year friendship isn't easily filled. Who, I wondered, did he call now and ask, "What's my telephone number?"

"January 30, 1980. Late yesterday afternoon, when we were having a drink, Truman telephoned. He thought, or pretended to think, that he had a message Sandy had called him. Again he asked nothing about us, and this time talked (briefly) only about his social plans—going in a few days to visit Jack in Verbier, then to Venice. 'I'll drink a Coca-Cola for you at Harry's Bar.'"

Another four months passed. As depressed as I was by all that had happened, I had not yet given up hope. Then Truman delivered the coup de grâce.

"June 4. Fire Island. On the train coming out here yesterday I picked up a *Daily News*. The first item in Liz Smith's column had my name in it, just the quote about success being a shy mouse from the *Letters* and 'wrote Tennessee Williams to Donald Windham in 1943.'

"Last night between seven and eight the phone rang. 'Hello, Donnie, it's Truman.'

"He asked if I'd seen the item, offered to read it to me, and went into his usual story of just being back from California, choosing a director for the movie of his story 'Handcarved Coffins,' 'which I guess you didn't see,' and: 'I think a foreign director would be best, Miloš Forman, but he's busy doing that picture by that man.' Then he informed me that he is dedicating his book which is about to come out, *Music for Chameleons*, to Tennessee. I'm not quite sure that he exactly repeated his printed statement about how good Tennessee was to him during his 'illness' (I'm not quite sure of how any of the conversation went after a certain point), but he expanded on it, telling me what a moving 'seven-page' letter Tennessee had written him. In response I let out enough of what I feel about Tennessee, including that I prefer not even to speak to anyone who has anything to do with him ('I can understand, after the way he treated you.') and Dotson Rader, asking how his friend Rader is ('I haven't seen Dotson Rader for five years.'), for him to start drawing the conversation to a close. As a part of the windup he asked how Sandy was, and Sandy, listening from across the room and aware, as I guess Truman is incapable of being now, of how upset I was by Truman's call, said he would come and speak to him. Truman began with him as he had begun with me, buddy, buddy, but Sandy told him to leave us alone and not to call anymore, adding, 'Do you understand?' ('Yes.') And: 'Is there anything else you want before we hang up?' ('Yes, I want to speak to Donnie again.') My reserve burst when I got back on the phone and I don't know what all I said (I did say that I hadn't known what Sandy was going to say to him), but it poured out from all the hurt I've stored up in the last year and a half and included how it had wounded me to read his saying in an article how Tennessee had been so good to him in his 'illness' and what great friends they were. As I remember, he started to defend himself, then thought better of it and ended the conversation with a businesslike matter of factness. I was completely undone, my hands and body shaking and jerking, my teeth chattering, words and sobs coming out beyond my control. Today I don't know whether I regret having revealed my feelings or not. It probably won't mean anything to Truman either way. Anyway, Sandy gave me a short drink of 150-proof rum and got me to bed."

"July 12. Saw Capote's book in Doubleday's: 'For Tennessee Williams.'"

"August 5. Truman on the *Today* show: very sad, very pitiful, very clear he hasn't stopped drinking."

"August 21. Truman on the Dick Cavett program: the inventor of the non-falsehood lie; it's true 'because it amuses me more that way.'"

"August 24. A remark of Truman's on TV, quoting Camus ('the little bit I've told and they're already yelling') has had the slightly delayed effect of turning me to Camus's books, which I haven't had off the shelf for a while:

"'Each artist thus keeps in his heart of hearts a single stream which, so long as he is alive, feeds what he is and what he says. When the stream runs dry, you see his work gradually shrivel up and start to crack. These are the wastelands of art which the invisible current has ceased to feed. His hair thin and dry, the artist, a field of stubble, is ripe for silence. . . .' Preface to *L'Envers et l'Endroit.*"

"December 1. Two years since we've seen Truman."

"December 1, 1981. Three years since we've seen Truman."

"December 1, 1982. Four years since we've seen Truman."

New York, June–December 1982*

---

*Capote died in August 1984 without my ever having seen or spoken to him again.

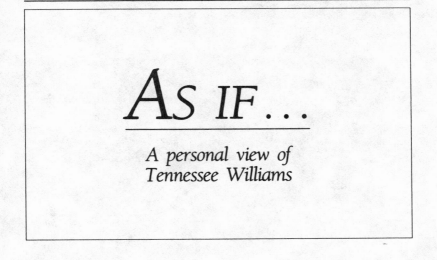

AS IF...

A personal view of
Tennessee Williams

"though not with bag and baggage, yet with scrip and scrippage"

—William Shakespeare, *As You Like It*

Caricature by Fred Melton, New York, 1940

ONE

"For the dead, who seem to take away so much, really take with them nothing that is ours. The passion they have aroused lives after them, easy to transmute or to transfer, but well-nigh impossible to destroy."

—E. M. Forster, *Where Angels Fear to Tread*

· 1 ·

When Tennessee Williams died I remembered the wild whoop of laughter with which, when I first knew him, he greeted this item in a newpaper: an old man in a wheelchair had been set afire and burnt to death when he fell asleep with his lit cigar in his mouth. Reading of Tennessee's death, I thought of the equal whoop of laughter with which in those days he would have greeted the news that a famous playwright, of renown such as his, and with a forty-year history of announcing his impending demise from heart trouble, had died by choking to death on a plastic bottle top.

And I thought of the different quality his laughter would have had in the later days. When I first knew him he would have been laughing at life *and himself*—himself and life having been one for him then, in a manner and to a degree not usually seen or recognized. I thought of how in the later days he and life had become peculiarly separated and opposed. And the early laughter lost. But again, in a manner that, although often seen, is not often recognized.

Tennessee's humor was frequently inexplicable. I, nevertheless, always found it infectious. Once he went to a play and came back roaring with amusement. A character on entering had said, "I'm Swiss!" And as Tennessee quoted the words he shouted with a louder guffaw than ever, repeating the line over and over. Later in the play another character, hearing an offstage noise, had whispered, "That *could* be a door slamming—or a body falling downstairs." And for months afterward Tennessee, breaking into a bizarre horselaugh, would cry out, "I'm Swiss!" and reduce both of us to irrepressible mirth. Or when any daily event was suspicious or uncertain, he would roll his eyes to heaven and warn, "That *could* be a door slamming—or a body falling downstairs," and go off into equally infectious gales of hee-hees.

Leaving aside the inexplicableness of Tennessee's humor in those days, it went hand in hand with an extraordinary dedication to writing. This unlikely combination of traits disconcerted many people. Those who knew the person first didn't want to believe that he could be a serious artist. Those who admired the work and then met Tennessee were equally perturbed. Many people looked gravely askance at his humor even in his drama and fiction. They saw nothing funny, only unpleasantness, in a play such as 27 Wagons Full of Cotton, no poetry only morbidity, in a story such as "Desire and the Black Masseur." They were offended in personal encounters by his laughing at the near and moving tragedy of his sister's madness. They did not understand his hilarity at such incidents as that of the old man in the wheelchair. His unlikely combination of traits in those days embodied Thoreau's designation of humor as the indispensable pledge of sanity: Tennessee looked at life then with the distant view of comedy, rather than with the near view of tragedy, because his personal tragedies were so close to the center of his emotions that, to preserve his saneness, he had to look at them as if they were far off.

This combination of humor and seriousness resulted in some extreme reactions. Mary Hunter,* an early admirer of Tennessee's work, was negotiating to produce You Touched Me at the time he finished 27 Wagons Full of Cotton. When he gave her the short play to read, she was offended. She thought he was trying to pull some inexplicable joke on her: she refused to believe it when both he and I protested that the intention of the short play, as of the long one, was comic. Later, when 27 Wagons was given its first performance in a workshop production, Maureen Stapleton played the role of Flora. She performed it exactly as Tennessee had intended and was reduced to tears because the audience laughed at her performance. It had not occurred to her that the condensed emotions of the material demanded the relief of laughter. Mutual acquaintances warned me that anyone who could greet tragedies with the humor Tennessee could was not a

*Who, with Jerome Robbins, Horton Foote and others, all at the start of their careers, had formed the American Actors Company.

person with a decent character *or* a sense of humor, and advised me that he was to be steered clear of, not joined in his laughter.

After Tennessee's death, thinking of those early years and the changes in the later ones, I remembered the comment of Jessica Tandy, who said that she did not feel so much sorrow that Tennessee had died as joy that he had lived. And I realized that in my thoughts the old Tennessee had died but not the young one. For me the Tennessee of the last decades had lost the immortal quality the youthful Tennessee had possessed. Over the years I had watched a unique person—the most individual of individuals—changed into a type. I had observed the distinguishing characteristics that had set him apart transformed by time and circumstances into the cliché traits of so many artists who become the victims rather than the heroes of their fates. But, in the face of eternity, of "something that goes on and on when life and death and time and everything else is all through with,"* this did not cancel the joy there had been.

In the months following Tennessee's death, various people approached me wanting me to help them with information for the biographies they were undertaking. My encounters with Tennessee in the last years had been sufficiently unpleasant for me to be depressed at the idea of talking about him to people who had not known him, or who had known him only in the last decades, and who considered us, or knew that others had considered us, enemies. I felt that without an emotional necessity to understand, which demanded the facing of all the contradictions and confusions, there was little chance that these biographers would recognize the complexity of the task they had undertaken or of the enigma they had set out to put down in words. At the prospect of trying to make this clear, I realized that I myself, despite the emotional necessity I felt, had never faced all the unanswered questions.

In the various essays I made to describe Tennessee while he was alive, I never allowed myself to go all the way to the end of trying to understand these inexplicable—insofar as I was willing to go—contradictions. As long as both of us were living I wanted to keep open the possibility of connection and com-

*From the prologue to *Summer and Smoke*. All other quoted phrases not otherwise identified are from Tennessee's writing.

munication. Writing about a playwright with Tennessee's problems in *The Hero Continues*, I rejected advice that I should make my novel a *roman à clef*; editing and annotating *Tennessee Williams' Letters to Donald Windham*, I avoided going beyond the necessities of friendly explanations. It is true that in my mentions of Tennessee in "Footnote to a Friendship," I treated him with less indulgence, having learned that indulgence did not pacify the person I hoped to reach. But I still held back, aware that any time I happened to reveal one of the truths Tennessee knew about himself, I ran the risk of augmenting his compulsion to conceal his knowledge from others by passing it off as the hostile opinion of an enemy. But now the book of possibilities is closed.

In the later years I realized that an extraordinary change had taken place in Tennessee shortly before we met in New York in January 1940. But I had no idea of it at the time. I thought then that his character and manner must have always been as they were. At nineteen, I had little preconception of what people were apt to be like. Nevertheless, I was aware as soon as I met him that Tennessee was different from anyone else I knew. His disconcerting seriousness and sense of humor were obvious. They also seemed to be innate. And when I discovered much later that there had been a recent change behind his striking characteristics of 1940, I still did not question the nature of this change. It is only since his death that I have come to a conclusion of what its nature was. And it is only in the last months, wondering what his biographers will make of the facts they gather, that I have realized this conclusion is the only one that, unlike my earlier rationalizations, which often brought up as many questions as they answered, solves the riddles that have appeared one after another throughout the years.

Secondhand information about Tennessee's early life (information accompanied by a full retinue of misinformation) was well in evidence by the time he published his *Memoirs* in 1975. It was apparent by then that up until about a year before I met him, the person who had been known as Thomas Lanier Williams had been to all visible intents and purposes a wholly different character from the one I met. The most surprising difference was that his early writings were in no way exceptional. The story set in ancient Egypt that he had published in *Weird Tales* in his teens was commonplace. The plays he had written in the three colleges he attended up until the late age of twenty-seven were routine imitations of the then popular successes, also on subjects he knew nothing about, Hollywood producers, Pennsylvania prisoners, Alabama coal miners.

The same ordinariness appears to have been true of his observable behavior. He was a joiner, of fraternities and little-theater groups. Between terms at college, he formed a poetry workshop with other young students. Conformist in his desire to emulate the popular youths in his classes and neighborhood, he was conventionally ambitious and vain. At the same time, he was primly shy. Early photographs lend credence to what seemed to me in the 1940s his doubtful claim (hard to believe because there was nothing precise or finicky about him then) that his father used to call him "Miss Nancy." In the pictures from his late teens and early twenties he is a smooth-faced and unsmiling youth dressed as though for Sunday school or the senior prom. His serious, dark eyes are sweetly direct. His hair is unruffled, his necktie knotted as though it has just been straightened by his mother. Alone or with others, he has the air of the son of the family, who swims at the country club, points out to his parents the advantages of being a "frat man," and mails his laundry home from college.

Aside from one or two of his leg-pulling, Rabelaisian (and heterosexual) fantasies, his and other people's reminiscences portray him as a virgin through his college years, totally repressed insofar as giving any expression to his libidinous desires is concerned.

The person I met in 1940 was a loner. A milky white cataract covered his divergent left eye. This walleye was as noticeable as a birthmark; but, accompanied by his rakish smile, it gave, instead, the impression of a continual, conspiratorial wink. Emulating no one I had ever seen other than a matinée idol in a movie, he smoked cigarettes in a long black holder. Clasping it before him as he talked, he looked provocatively into your eyes.

While still conversing, he let his focus fade to unseeing and, with a tap of his finger, knocked the cigarette ashes in your direction, as though no longer aware of your presence.

His clothes retained some resemblance to those of the youth in the early photographs. There was a collegiate jauntiness and lack of restraint in his sartorial manner. Looking younger than his twenty-eight years, he was visibly better off financially than most of my friends and I were. He boasted a whole wardrobe of footwear: dress oxfords, fashionable loafers, black-and-white saddle shoes. Alternating with his appearance of an innocent outsider, ready for rather than finished with college, he sported three-piece business suits, four-in-hand and bow neckties, a folded handkerchief in his jacket's breast pocket. But there was always something askew. Something that didn't fit. The tie and shirt clashed. Or he wore no socks. He was clean-shaven, as in his teens. But his hair was unruly; it was even kinky, despite his continual use of hair tonic and a bathing cap when he swam.

Usually as free as if it were his first night in town (which it often was, with his nomadic comings and goings), he was humbly eager for companionship. At the same time, he was invariably busy. He presented the social enigma of someone unaware of the difference between being alone and with others. When he was not on the make and trying to charm, his behavior frequently suggested that he had never been a part of any family, and certainly never under the supervision of a punctilious mother who was a regent of the D.A.R. At table, he appreciatively sucked his teeth. He smacked his lips and licked the food from around his mouth. He ate at any hour, whenever he was hungry, and always with an air of slight surprise that whoever he was with did not think it the inevitable eating time.

On his way to an appointment with his agent or the producers who were interested in his plays, he would catch sight of a cafeteria and say, "I think I'll have a rice pudding." Entering, he would eat a bowl of soup or a plate of chicken croquettes. Reminded of his appointment, he would reply, "Oh, I don't imagine they'll be expecting me now," and suggest returning to the YMCA, where he was staying, for a swim. Arrived at the Y, he would sit down at his typewriter to work.

As for being sexually repressed, the evening I met him and

throughout the first years of our acquaintance, his quotidian goal was to end up in bed with a partner at least once before the twenty-four hours was over.

If he was shy, he was equally bold. His practice in a room of half a dozen more or less presentable males was to make a pass at the one he found most attractive and then, if it was not successful, to go on down the line. The forwardness of his advances frequently produced disillusions in the young men who thought some irresistible attraction of their own inspired his ardor. If none of these approaches was successful, there were still the showers and steam rooms at the Y. In his room, amid the disordered contents of his suitcase and footlocker trunk, he kept, besides a jar of Vaseline, a bottle of Cuprex, against crabs, and a tube of prophylactic salve, against gonorrhea. A small drawstring bag, like the bags cigarette tobacco was sold in then, accompanied the tube of salve, to tie around his genitals and protect his clothing when he dressed after the salve was applied.

Also in the suitcase and trunk, and all over the bed, were piles of manuscript. This juxtaposition was not incidental. His attitude toward his work shared the same disordered concentration and emphasis on release as his attitude toward sex. There was no longer anything impersonal about his writing.

In 1939, he had published "The Field of Blue Children," a story whose subject was the frustrated romance between a boy and a girl, members of the poetry club at a Midwestern college. But by the time I met him he had gone beyond exploring the outer material of the subject matter he knew. He was pouring forth his innermost feelings. And by then he had an uncanny ability to project his emotions into any situation or character whose reality or fantasy he responded to, an ability so unpredicted in his earlier efforts that he might have sold his soul to the devil for it. He was writing incantatory stories, "The Malediction," "Desire and the Black Masseur," psychologically distinct plays, *Portrait of a Madonna*, *The Last of My Solid Gold Watches*. Even in his poetry, primitive and conventional in form, there was no longer anything cautious or conformist. There was, rather, an apparently childish lack of self-consciousness or prosody.

And, of course, he had changed his name. Not only profes-

sionally—even if the impetus was for professional protection—
but personally. Even then, he offered the explanation that he
signed his new work Tennessee because he did not want it asso-
ciated with the juvenile poetry he had published as Thomas
Lanier Williams. But he gave no hint that Tennessee was not a
nickname by which old friends had for years been accustomed
to call him. None of his new acquaintances in New York knew
that it was a name he had devised on his own when, at twenty-
seven, he entered the Group Theatre contest for new playwrights
twenty-five years of age and younger. None of us was aware of
the items, which had appeared over the previous years in St.
Louis newspapers when as Thomas Lanier Williams he won local poetry and playwriting contests, and which gave his correct
age. All we knew was that in New York he presented himself to
one and all as Tennessee. His intimate name was Tenn. And if
he was feeling particularly close to you, he signed his letters 10.

From the time he left home, "Tennessee" never lacked invention.

· 2 ·

In those years Tennessee was—at least he thought of himself as being—romantic and cynical. When we met he attributed these qualities to me. The intensity of my attachment to the friend I had come to New York with, and the unhesitatingness of my rejections, interested him. But it disconcerted him that I thought things out and made choices I stuck to. I lacked the romantic illusion that one could have things both ways. I expected nothing from what wasn't important to me. And what did not touch my heart I ignored. I wanted to be with the person I loved. And I wanted to be a writer. But I had no conception of writing as a "career," the way Tennessee did. When I discovered that, despite his standard of aesthetic integrity, he was cannily inscribing dedications to Helen Hayes, Lillian Gish, and Sydney Greenstreet on the typescripts of his one-act plays, my surprise equalled my admiration.

Fred Melton and I had arrived from Atlanta shortly before, knowing no one in New York. We had come with one suitcase each, and with the meager money we had saved in the previous year from his job as a sign painter in a department store and mine as a laborer in a barrel factory. Tennessee, who had arrived as the winner of second prize in the Group Theatre contest, as well as the recipient of a one-thousand-dollar Rockefeller Foundation grant, was impressed by our improvidence.* It was our romantic two-against-the-world determination to stay together that attracted him. Similarly, it was his solitary vagabondage that made him heroic in my eyes. And although Tennessee's social life was largely determined then by his looking for someone to go to bed with, and this was not to happen with Melton or me,

*And in an emergency he could get money from home, which neither Melton nor I could.

the three of us had become friends by the time he left a month later for St. Louis.

The middle of March he was back in New York. It was during this second installment of our friendship that I became aware of another of his distinctive traits: his prodigal habit of losing things. He arrived with a new plaid topcoat. The next week he lost it. The weather had turned warm, anyway, and following his dapper inclinations he fitted himself out with a new Panama hat and dark glasses. Easter Sunday the three of us went to the service at the Cathedral of St. John the Divine. The one-time-worn hat was left on the pew in the church.

Tennessee's birthday came during the week after Easter. Melton and I gave him a cigarette holder, which in those days he lost so regularly that he went through them almost as fast as he did cigarettes. Tennessee, for his part, gave us no hint that it was his twenty-ninth rather than his twenty-sixth birthday. It was not until almost five years later that I learned he lied about how old he was, when his mother on the opening night of *The Glass Menagerie* in Chicago looked into the program and said, "Why, son, this writeup has your age wrong."

A month after his birthday Tennessee left again. He had decided to head out to Mexico for the summer. The Sunday morning he was to depart he telephoned and asked us to come to the Y and help him pack. When we arrived he was kneeling on the floor in the middle of the room surrounded by so great a chaos that it looked as though he were moving out of a house where he had lived for years. On the verge of throwing in the towel, he was trying to sort his possessions into three groups—to put into a cardboard box, a suitcase, and a footlocker trunk. His clothes were already packed. But the desk and chest, the bed and windowsill, were cluttered with manuscripts. His dilemma was which to discard, which to pack and leave in St. Louis, which to take with him.

From among the pages as he sorted, he produced copies of *Partisan Review, Time, New Masses, Look.* He offered these to us, along with various toilet articles that he removed from the suitcase to make room for manuscripts. Also into the suitcase went his copy of the *Collected Poems of Hart Crane,* over which only the manuscripts took precedence and which, despite his easy references to his father and mother, his sister and brother, seemed in those days to be his real family. When he finished, he and Melton tied up the cardboard box with cord. Then the three of us—carrying the box, the suitcase, the trunk, his portable typewriter, his rented radio to return for the deposit, his several coats, an envelope of short stories and one-act plays for me to deliver the next morning to the Liebling-Wood office in Radio City—trooped down to the lobby for him to pay his bill.

At the monumental old Pennsylvania Station he spent a long time in the marble waiting room buying his ticket and checking his luggage. Then we went upstairs to the Clover Bar and Tennessee bought us farewell drinks. We would not see each other again for the summer—and, with our uncertain lives, who knew for how much longer. To underline the importance of his departure, he had telephoned an acquaintance from St. Louis and asked her, also, to see him off. When she arrived he made introductions; then he left the conversation to the three of us, while he sat, in what I already recognized as one of his habitual social attitudes, detached and smiling into space to cover up the fact that, whatever importance the occasion might have, his attention was not on the events going on around him.

Two weeks later he was back in town. He had gotten as far as Memphis to visit his grandparents when he received a telegram saying that the Theatre Guild was optioning *Battle of Angels*. But his ambivalent feeling about New York was already established, his fear of it as the place which was arbiter of giving or withholding what he wanted, the place in which he was aware of as yet having no real importance and, more disagreeably, the place which had the patriarchal power to judge him as he felt his father had judged him in his youth. He left almost immediately for Lake George, where he had been told the swimming was good.

In the meantime I had started working at the World's Fair in Flushing, selling Coca-Cola, and Melton in the office of an architect on East Thirty-seventh Street. It was there, across the street in the same block, that he saw a sign offering a duplex apartment for sublet for the summer. Tennessee, once more in town—having found to his surprise that the water in upstate

New York lakes was cold in May—agreed to rent the apartment with us. We moved in the first of June.

Tennessee took the top floor, one large studio, three windows wide, with striped awnings over the windows. In the middle, under a skylight, stood a large table. There was also, besides a daybed, a rented piano. Neither Melton nor I could play it; but Tennessee, who could pick out a few tunes, decided to keep it and declared that he would pay the rent. What he played, however, was the wind-up Victrola he had begun to travel with, adding a Sadie Thompson touch to his assorted equipment. While he worked at the large table, the Victrola ground out "La Golondrina," or Dietrich singing "I've Been in Love Before." The sound gradually slowed and faded as the spring ran down until the slurred words were replaced by the steady clatter of his typing. In his pauses to think, he cracked his knuckles, first of his right hand, then of the left. Or put a cigarette in his holder. When he noticed the silence, he wound up the Victrola again.

I had already become aware from the evidence in his rooms at the Y of Tennessee's method of work. But it was while we were sharing the apartment that I became aware of its full fury. It was there that I first read, as well as the finished stories and plays he was giving to his agent, the poems, stories and plays he was working on, writing and rewriting, day after day. And it was there, in the large studio, which he soon made as disordered as he had the small cubbyholes at the Y, that I learned there was nothing any more cautious or conventional about his method of writing than there was about the finished product.

Revising a short story or a one-act play, he didn't correct the latest version. He tossed it aside and, with a concentration that made him oblivious of everything outside himself, rewrote from the beginning. Not once, but over and over. Sometimes the changes he made were enrichments, verbal and thematic, of what was already there. Sometimes he was so carried away by new inspirations and releases of emotion that the revision was in effect a new story on the same theme.

For each of these revisions Tennessee held in, often for phenomenal lengths of time, everything in his backlog of emotions that was seeking release, everything he felt, until he could rush through it blindly, furiously, to a climax of achievement.

The resulting richness of words was often extraordinary. In the early 1940s, Sandy Campbell and a young actress were performing *This Property is Condemned* in acting class for the Russian director Theodore Komisarjevsky. He asked who the author was. Sandy, pleased that the play interested the director, whose sister had created the role of Nina in *The Seagull,* explained and added, "He's like Chekhov, isn't he?" "No," Komisarjevsky replied. "Chekhov condenses. This man expands. He uses words the way Shakespeare uses words."

The richness of words in Tennessee's short stories and plays of the 1940s is not a richness of vocabulary. It is a richness of verbal texture. The richness of the warp and woof of the phrases that contain the emotions expressed, the characters and events presented. There are a good many metaphors and similes; but they are always, even when physically descriptive, used to reveal an inner state. They are used to draw the reader or listener into the author's emotions, not to display his intellect. Reading these stories and plays, I was aware that Tennessee was less interested in what he saw than in what he felt; but I was also aware that he saw a great deal more than I had realized, even though he seemed capable of refusing to see whatever conflicted with his feelings.

And it was while we were sharing the duplex apartment that I received the first of the clues to understanding the complicated, concealed, and never directly expressed elements in Tennessee's character. This happened after he had once more departed town and returned. For even after he had taken the apartment with us, his restless comings and goings did not cease. Toward the end of June he went to Cape Cod. It was there, on Captain Jack's Wharf in Provincetown, that he met Kip Kiernan.

Kip was a Hanya Holm dance student who posed for life classes at Hans Hofmann's painting school. Tennessee's sexual and emotional involvement with him, from beginning to end, lasted six weeks. On Tennessee's first trip back to New York, he brought with him a small clay head he had modeled of Kip, with his pug nose, slanted eyes, and high cheekbones. He described Kip's figure, like Nijinsky's, and his beautiful buttocks. At the end of July he wrote a poetic letter extolling the details of their lovemaking and his emotions. In it he made the declaration that he knew Kip loved him, that nobody had ever loved him so completely, and he added for me to keep the letter carefully: it was only for people like "us," who had gone beyond shame.

It was this sentence that struck me at the time. His assumption about me was wrong: I had not gone beyond feeling shame about sex, I had never felt it; and despite the evidence I had seen in Tennessee's compulsive promiscuity and his ever-ready prophylactic salve, as though the punishment of disease was the most likely follow-up to the act of making love, it had not occurred to me that shame was for him an inevitable part of sex, which could only be either felt or passed beyond.

The middle of August, Tennessee fled from his affair with Kip. First to New York and then to Mexico—leaving unpaid his share of the rent on the apartment, as well as the sums due on the piano and on his rented portable typewriter, which he took with him. By then, his attitude had changed from the statement that Kip loved him as no one had ever loved him before to the complaint that Kip didn't love him enough; Kip was interested in a girl at the other end of the wharf. Even at the time, I thought he was fleeing from a fear of emotional commitment; and I asked myself why he was afraid of the presence of love; but if I gave myself an answer it may well have been any of a number of limited answers. I did not apply this clue to the overall picture, beyond the context of the summer. I had, in fact, very little picture to apply it to, and very little need to apply it.

· 3 ·

A series of snapshots from those years when Tennessee and life were peculiarly one.

He has returned in November for the rehearsals of the Theatre Guild's production of *Battle of Angels*. As he feels is suited to his new position, he has taken a room not at the Y but nearby on West Fifty-eighth Street, in the shabbily elegant apartment of a titled woman. Perhaps in honor of Miriam Hopkins, who is playing the lead in his play, he has added jodhpurs to his cigarette holder. He looks very Hollywood horsy set. One Saturday afternoon before the company leaves for Boston, he gives a small cocktail party in his room. The half-dozen guests are all as obscure as Melton and me. Tennessee himself is not present. There is a pint of whiskey on the mantel and a message for us to help ourselves. He will be late. I do not remember how long we stayed. However long it was, he never arrived. And the strength of my admiration was such that the incident made him only that much more marvelous—i.e., a marvel—in my eyes.

A year later. A painter's white-walled apartment in Greenwich Village. The Guild has closed *Battle of Angels* in Boston. Tennessee has returned to New York for a cataract operation, then gone to Key West to revise the play. Despite the fact that the Guild has rejected the revision, he has spent a happy summer in Provincetown, writing a pell-mell series of poems and a new play in blank verse. Now it is midwinter. The money that for the last year and a half has been easy come, easy go, is gone. Eliminating the paying of rent from his expenses, he is staying in the apartment of this new friend from Provincetown, Fritz Bultman. Determined not to take a job that will prevent him from devoting his days to writing, he is working nights as a poetry-reciting waiter at Valeska Gert's Beggars Bar in the Village. He declaims in the evenings the poems he writes in the afternoons. He has undergone a second cataract operation and to his increasingly Bohemian wardrobe has added a black eye-patch with a surrealist white eye painted on it. Almost daily, when he sits down at his typewriter in his host's spick-and-span apartment, after lighting a cigarette and putting the coffeepot on the stove to heat, he pauses and wonders if there is a fire in the neighborhood that accounts for the odor of burning. This destruction of coffeepots does not add to his charm as a guest. One afternoon when I stop by the apartment to see him, he tells me that his host is too persnickety. He is leaving.

Early next spring. My room in the West Sixty-third Street Y. Tennessee and I are laughing at the impossibility of our situations. Melton, who has joined the Coast Guard but is stationed on shore duty, has married a girl from Georgia and I have moved here. Tennessee by this time is without sufficient funds to rent a room even if he wants to. Life, he says, his mood sobering, is not livable without money; he can no longer face the prospect of this grubbing existence.

His appearance has retreated from its Bohemian phase to a threadbare revival of the dapper manner he dressed in when we met. For the first time since I have known him, he is living not merely in someone else's apartment but *with* someone. The man he is sleeping with is a songwriter. He is not only older than Tennessee but—more important—more affluent. Tennessee has gone to his apartment to spend the evening and, faced with an invitation to stay on, found it the least impossible of alternatives. For one night, there are no two ways about it from Tennessee's viewpoint: sex is sex. And although it is one of the facts he is least likely to face straightforwardly, Tennessee is attractive to what he invariably calls "old aunties," however near to his own age and masculinity the person in question may be. He is vain about it. The unacceptable thing to him is not to be the arbiter. The insidious thing is for some necessity beyond that of his own desire to enter. The shameful thing is other people's desires. And he makes a most expressive grimace of disgust when he mentions them. Just as he makes a most gleeful rolling of his eyes to heaven when he mentions his own. In no time, he has come to feel that he is trapped in a nightmare at the songwriter's apartment in a townhouse in the East Fifties. Daily, he crosses to the Y and joins me in my room. We are working on a dramatization of D.H. Lawrence's short story "You Touched Me," which I have begun in the hope of making money and which he says can be made more commercial with his help. The more financial irons in the fire the better. He looks upon his escaping here to work, and to put on my robe and go down to the pool to swim, as a desperate flight to a temporary refuge.

Today's entrance is particularly dramatic. Dropping his mangy topcoat to the floor, he recounts the fagging night he has passed with the songwriter and his alcoholic friends and vows that he could not have survived it without my companionship to look forward to. For my part, I welcome his company as an escape from loneliness and my feeling of having lost my direction in life; or, more accurately, his company makes me feel that I have a comrade in the only direction in life that is left to me, that of being a writer.

Thanksgiving of that year. Tennessee and I are staying in Melton's apartment in the Village, a dark, semibasement room with a large, dusty garden. He and his wife have moved here from the sunny, top-floor apartment where he and I lived. After leaving the songwriter's, Tennessee has spent the summer in Georgia. Then he has worked for two months for the War Department in Florida, operating a teletype machine on a night shift, enjoying the wild, wartime life of Jacksonville almost as much as he did his carefree summers in Provincetown. Now there is a chance that You Touched Me will be produced; he has quit his job and returned to New York. We are making one more revision of the play. He arrived, as usual, with very little money, barely enough for a cheap room. Then Melton, who was leaving with his wife for a trip south to see her family, said Tennessee could live in their place while they were gone—but only if I stayed there with him to protect it. So one day after work I went to Tennessee's room and helped him move his battered luggage, now almost completely stuffed with manuscripts, downtown. Since the summer I have left the Y and been living in the apartment of a friend in the next block from Melton's. I, too, have a new job, working in an office at the School of American Ballet, helping Lincoln Kirstein edit *Dance Index* magazine.

This morning Melton has returned, leaving his wife in Georgia a week longer. When he learns that I am not planning for us to spend this week together in the apartment with Tennessee just as though he has never married, he sulks. I walk out. Before I reach the corner, Tennessee comes after me: Melton has gone berserk and begun busting up the apartment.

"What am I going to do?" he asks frantically. "All of my manuscripts are in there!"

I tell him to fetch them and come with me.

"If I try to get them it will just draw his attention to them. That's my life's work in there, Donnie. You've got to come back with me. There's no telling what he'll do in the state he's in."

I return with him, but wait at the entrance. It seems a long time before he comes out, lugging his bulging suitcases. As we carry his manuscripts to the next block, he tells me that Melton has smashed his fist through a glass pane of the door to the garden and cut himself.

The manuscripts safe, we go back. Tennessee has torn up his last clean shirt and tied it around Melton's hand. I take Melton to the Naval Hospital on Hudson Street. When he comes out, everything is all right. We walk up the street through the autumn sunshine, his arm around me, and laugh at how frightened Tennessee was for his manuscripts. We spend the afternoon cleaning up the apartment. In the evening, he and I and Tennessee take the Fifth Avenue bus uptown to Kirstein's, where we have been invited to Thanksgiving dinner. The next morning Tennessee moves to the Y.

A collage of succeeding events.

The producer likes the play less after the revision. The year ends with Tennessee's money gone again. But he holds out. Pursuing the goal he has in mind, he dares not stoop to comfort. A new friend at the Y helps him to decamp without paying his rent. The two of them sneak his suitcases down a back staircase and out a service entrance. He moves to a cheap hotel a block further uptown, visible from his room at the Y, which has attracted his attention with its symbolic reproduction of the Statue of Liberty overlooking its roof.

But this freedom is illusory. His appearance changes once more. His makeshift wardrobe descends toward a skid-row look. His clothes seem as though he has slept in them. He catches a chest cold and spits into bits of toilet tissue he stuffs into his pockets. His beard always looks two days old.

He confides in me that a doctor has told him his heart is dangerously enlarged, "as big as a baby's head," and warned him that he should go up stairs by putting both feet on each step: it is better to reach the top slowly than not to reach it at all. Whenever anyone invites me to dinner, I ask if I can bring him along. When I get my twenty-five-dollar salary each Friday, we eat together.

Almost every time he gets on the subway he boards the wrong train and ends up in Brooklyn Heights. Hoping to baffle this fate, he moves for a week to the St. George Hotel, at the Brooklyn Heights stop of the Seventh Avenue subway. His enthusiasm for sex hasn't changed. On weekends, he is cleanshaven and we usually scrape together enough money for a few beers in the serviceman-filled Crossroads Bar at the Times Square stop of the same subway.

His typewriter having been sold, along with every other disposable possession, he comes daily to the *Dance Index* office to use the extra typewriter there. Kirstein, getting used to seeing him typing poems each time he looks in, offers to submit his poetry to James Laughlin at New Directions. As 1943 begins, Tennessee enters his few weeks of menial employment in Manhattan. He takes a job operating an elevator at a hotel off Madison Avenue. Fired, he works as an usher at the Strand Theatre on Broadway. Finally, extracting through his agent, Audrey Wood, bus fare from a producer who is considering his play *Stairs to the Roof,* he makes the move he has been avoiding for so long. He goes home to St. Louis.

The first week of May. Tennessee has returned and I am again seeing him off on a train at Pennsylvania Station. Spring sunlight falls through the steel and glass spiderweb of the dome.

Except for Audrey Wood, who has negotiated a $250-a-week contract for him as a writer at Metro-Goldwyn-Mayer, there are only the two of us. His other contacts in New York have been queered or exhausted during the last months. There are no attendant players to swell his progress, as there will be beginning a year and a half later, when he departs from the same place for Chicago with the company of *The Glass Menagerie*. Nor is there any standing in line to buy his ticket. Everything has been taken care of, including his Pullman compartment. With his new affluence he has less luggage. His cache of manuscripts remains stored at the *Dance Index* office, where he left them when he went to St. Louis, asking me to consider myself his literary executor. The only visible addition to his paraphernalia is the mint copy of the best-selling historical novel he has been hired to adapt. Clasping it awkwardly, an object he does not want and does not know what to do with, he resembles a child with a primer on the first day of school. Or, rather, fitted out in his best suit, a child with a missal on his way to Sunday School. He looks as youthful as he did when I first knew him. And more innocent. He is, in fact, frightened. And after Audrey leaves he keeps repeating that when he is settled I must come and visit him. Together, we will have a good time in California. The next morning from Chicago, where he has a layover to change to the Super Chieftain for the West Coast, he writes a hasty note to me on a museum catalog, holding on until the last to a familiarity he knows to be friendly and admiring. When he reaches Hollywood he will be judged by the studio moguls who, even more than the theatrical establishment of New York, will evaluate him coldly. Through their wealth and his poverty they have had the power to seduce him from the path to his solitary goal. At $250 a week, the job he has taken can hardly be called a stooping to comfort; but it is no nearer to the end he is seeking than working a teletype machine or running an elevator. It is less near than the writing of poems or the spending of a summer on a play in blank verse.

And in no time, he discovers that despite his fears his studio job separates him no further from his goal than did those other makeshift employments. In no time, he is spending his days as always, not only in his apartment at Santa Monica but in his office at the studio, behind the locked door, working on his own writing, alert to his own emotions, vague to all else, and in the evenings savoring, if not Hollywood itself, the joys of the Palisades nights of Santa Monica, just as earlier he had savored the Ocean Street evenings of Jacksonville.

· 4 ·

A parenthesis.

Midway during the six months that Tennessee worked at MGM, he wrote me a letter referring to the announcements of two upcoming little-theater productions of *You Touched Me* in which he was listed as sole author. Instead of being concerned that my name was omitted, he wrote, I should bear in mind that the preponderance of the work on the play was his and that his reputation was greater than mine. He had put his heart, labor, time and desperation into the script and it was fitting that he should receive the preponderance of the credit. Profits, of which there was no possibility in these productions, would be divided equally.

Rereading this letter in 1976, when I was editing the book of his correspondence with me, I wondered what my reaction had been when I received it. Hoping to find my reply, I wrote to the University of Texas and asked if any of my letters to Tennessee were among the voluminous papers he had deposited there. Told that there were none, I put this information in the book, in a footnote to the letter that had inspired my inquiry.

After the publication of the trade edition of the *Letters,* among the reviews was one that labeled me as "pernicious" for having preserved Tennessee's correspondence and the manuscripts of his plays he gave me. It stated that Tennessee "had always been indifferent to . . . manuscripts, letters, photos and the like." And it quoted him as protesting, "I never save personal letters. Why should I?"

The autumn after Tennessee's death, a writer who had been doing research at the University of Texas told me that among the manuscripts, letters, photos and the like in the Williams archive he had seen a stack of my letters to Tennessee. I wrote to the university: How could this be true in face of the information I had been given earlier? I was told that the reply to my previous request had been negative because at the time there had been no *catalogued* letters from me to Williams. The letters had arrived at the university on his instructions at the beginning of 1965, but they had been deposited in a sealed envelope with the contents unlisted and the restriction, dated May 1, 1964, that the envelope remain "sealed until the death of Tennessee Williams."

· 5 ·

My answer to Tennessee's 1943 letter from Santa Monica was among my correspondence in Texas. After agreeing that he had done the preponderance of the work on *You Touched Me* and that his reputation was greater than mine, my letter said:

"I have nothing to lose, everything to gain, by the coupling of our names—for that reason I hate to say too much. Naturally I want my name to come out with more value than it goes in, as when I grow enough I have a lot of writing of my own to do. Perhaps the main thing we have in common is that we both intend to devote our lives to writing and are not mainly interested in getting money out of it."*

When Tennessee finished *The Glass Menagerie,* which he was in the middle of his three years of writing and rewriting that summer in Santa Monica, it was the least commercially oriented of his scripts. That it would be optioned by a Broadway producer in 1944 was as unlikely as that it would be a success once it was produced. Even more unlikely was that its being cast unrealistically, as far as the ages of the actors were concerned, would enhance rather than diminish the artistry of the play. Most unlikely of all was that once the production was in rehearsal, faced with the director's and producer's determination to improve it with gags, Tennessee would be able to defend the integrity of the script. But he stood up to them with the courage

---

*It is worth saying here that whatever preponderance of the work on the play was Tennessee's, it was greatest at this point. He had added, over my expressed objections, two crude comic characters that I thought detrimental. One of them, with Mary Hunter's help when she was planning a production, I succeeded in removing before the Cleveland and Pasadena tryouts. The other was cut as soon as the play went into rehearsals for Guthrie McClintic's Broadway production in 1945.

that five years of battling the crassness of the commercial theater had bred in him.

Chicago. The night after Christmas, 1944. The Civic Theatre. Outside there is ice and a gale wind that pushes you back inside when you try to go out the door of a hotel or theater. I am elated, despite having sat up all night in a wartime crowded train coach from New York. Beside me is seated Tennessee's mother, imperturbable, the smiling regent of the D.A.R. She has come from St. Louis for the first performance of *Menagerie*. Tennessee, his nervousness increased by her presence, has wandered off before the curtain rose. The play unfolds, word for word as in the manuscript Tennessee gave me after the professional typist's copies were made. At the end of the final scene, however, in contrast to the direction in the script, and her performance at all rehearsals, including that afternoon's, Laurette Taylor does not exit. She has no intention of leaving the audience with a last view of only Eddie Dowling and Julie Haydon. The curtain falls on all three. Tennessee returns to take us backstage.

It has become part of the *Menagerie* legend that in her dressing room after the opening night in Chicago, Laurette Taylor asked Tennessee's mother, "Well, how did you like yourself, Mrs. Williams?" But I don't think it has been noted that Miss Taylor, who had not met Mrs. Williams before that night, based her performance of Amanda on her careful observation of Tennessee. Her sideways, suspicious glances at her children when she was displeased; her silences that spoke more than words; her bright obliviousness to the reality before her eyes when she was determined to show that she, at least, was agreeable; and her childish pleasure in the chance to charm and show off her best features when there was an opportunity to do so without jeopardizing her goal; even her sorghum Southern accent, which Tennessee innocently objected to as sounding like the Aunt Jemima Pancake Hour, were all recognizable to me as adaptations of mannerisms of Tennessee's. With inspiration, she saw that this was the best way to give external reality to the emotions the author of *Menagerie* had put into his words. She had watched Tennessee and sized him up, with years more experience of people of his complexity than I had.

New York. The thirty-first of March, 1945. A balmy spring night. Buds are out on the trees in Central Park. The air is milky, the breeze like a cool bedsheet against your face. Tennessee and I are walking about the damp side streets around Times Square. It is Easter eve, toward midnight. We have been together most of the day. After working in the morning at the *Dance Index* office, I have met him early in the afternoon. The two of us have searched the secondhand shops along Second and Third Avenues for a new lampshade required for the floor lamp in the second act of *Menagerie,* still not supplied by the producers six hours before the opening.

Tennessee, who had ceded all but two of his allotted tickets for the opening to Audrey Wood, took me with him. After the final curtain he was called to the stage with excited shouts of "Author, author!" But he is, at least on the surface, calmer than I am. As we walk about the half-deserted streets we talk of how much coughing there was during the performance. Was the audience bored, or is this the behavior of New York first-nighters? Will the critics, on whom everything depends, like the play? We stop in a bar and Tennessee suddenly remembers that Audrey has asked him to come to her suite at the Royalton for a drink after the show. Is it too late to go? Deciding that it isn't, he insists that I come with him. Seeing Audrey and her husband, Bill Liebling, alone makes him shy. But when we arrive the suite is filled with important theater people, Robert Edmond Jones, Edwin Justus Mayer, etc.

After the reviews appear on Monday, Tennessee retains his surface calm. Perhaps it is the numbness of shock. Wednesday morning I go to his room at the Shelton Hotel. He has invited me to lunch. A reporter from the *N. Y. Times* and two women photographers from *Life* are there. One asks him if he ever writes in bed. When he responds affirmatively, she instructs him to lie down, then flops his portable typewriter on top of him. After watching her arrange her camera and wait for him to start typing, he says apologetically, "When I work in bed, I usually write in longhand."

As soon as the photography session is over, he hurries off to be interviewed for *The New Yorker.* I am left to take to lunch a soldier friend of his who has turned up.

Despite Tennessee's defense of the script of *Menagerie,* he went along with anything in the way of promotion. He helped create legends and created them himself—as he had since the days when he made up the name Tennessee. It was publicity fodder from the start that he based the characters of Laura and Amanda on his sister and mother—although he himself later pointed out that there was very little of his sister in Laura. (There was more of himself, I would say.)* In truth, when he was writing the play, he neither intended nor considered it a transformed-but-essentially-truthful portrait of his early home life in St. Louis. But this is what he implied he had done in the article he wrote for the N.Y. *Herald Tribune* following the opening.

Tennessee called *Menagerie* a memory play. I would say that it is a dream play. The central fact of Tennessee's home life in St. Louis was the presence of his father. And although the elimination of a father from the Wingfield family can be explained as an act of wish fulfillment, the remaining characters in *Menagerie* are not in any family situation that, from my knowledge, Tennessee ever experienced. He worked for a period at the shoe company where his father was employed, but he did not contribute to the support of his family. He had heard from me and others of the times in our homes when the gas and electricity were turned off because the bills were not paid; but despite the early years in dreary apartments, these were not things he had experienced in the St. Louis houses, furnished with Oriental rugs, mahogany dining-room suites, a grand piano in the parlor, where his mother gave teas for the D.A.R., with ices, sandwiches and cakes from a caterer.

He borrowed whatever was useful, from any direction, from his own life and other's lives. And he carried this freehand appropriation over into his presentation of himself. I don't think

---

*For example, Laura has less kinship with the "my sister" than with the "I" of "The Resemblance Between a Violin Case and a Coffin." Her shy romantic attitude toward the gentleman caller is nearer to the brother's than to the sister's attraction to the boy in that much more autobiographical story.

anyone will ever know, for instance, how much he borrowed for himself—from Philip Horton's biography of Hart Crane—of Crane's love for his grandmother. This appropriation was another of the clues to his character that I didn't recognize until later. He assumed surrogate personalities, surrogate biographies, trying them on like suits of other people's clothes and substituting them for his own when they fitted the part he was playing, sometimes briefly, sometimes more or less permanently.

After Laurette Taylor's death, Tennessee used to talk about his and her love for each other. The times I was around them in Chicago and New York, I saw no manifestation of it. They were cautious and guarded with one another, not out of bafflement or dislike, as far as I could see, but out of recognition and self-protection. Each seemed to have an all-too-clear divination of what the other's character was like. I saw Laurette express her wariness of Tennessee only in sharp glances from her hooded eyes. But I saw a clearer, even though oblique, expression of Tennessee's distrust.

One evening a few weeks after the play had opened in New York, he and I went to a bar with the actor who played the gentleman caller. Also there were the stage manager and a group of backstage workers from *Menagerie*. They had asked to talk to Tennessee. An independent producer wanted to make a film of the play starring Miss Taylor. The money for the production was available; the task they were undertaking was to persuade Tennessee to agree to a percentage deal for the film rights. The producer could not offer him the extravagant advance he could get from Hollywood. On the other hand, no major studio would cast Laurette in its production. Her performance would be lost. A percentage deal, with success, could eventually bring Tennessee equal money. More important, he would have artistic control of the film script, and Laurette's performance would be preserved for posterity.

The group of us were sitting in a booth. As the conversation progressed, Tennessee became more and more silent. He puffed on the cigarette in his long black holder, frowning into space with a demeanor similar to, but recognizably different from, his demeanor when his thoughts were not on the events going on around him. Now and then, he responded, "Humm!" The meeting ended with Tennessee giving a series of nodded and grunted assents to the others' statements, but making none of his own. Afterward, knowing the extent of his admiration for Miss Taylor's performance, I asked why he had acted so suspicious. For the only time I can remember in those years, his lost his temper and turned on me.

"Don't you know why they're pressuring me about this?" he demanded angrily. "You're pretty naïve. They don't care about Laurette's performance or the play. They think that if I'll give this producer friend of theirs the rights they can all get themselves jobs with the film."

Later he told me that Audrey Wood was asking for the film rights to *Menagerie* the largest sum ever payed for a play.

· 6 ·

Tennessee's being hysterical at the New York openings of his plays, and his attributing his negative opinions of the plays to me, began in the 1950s.

He was calm and confident at the opening of *A Streetcar Named Desire,* as he had been during the rehearsals under Elia Kazan, rolling his eyes to heaven with humor. He was happy at the opening-night party and at the party he gave a short while later, in his furnished one-room apartment on East Thirty-sixth Street.

It took place the day after the blizzard of 1947. Traffic on the streets of New York had disappeared completely. The guests (including Greta Garbo) came by subway, if they did not walk through the empty white avenues, festively dotted with children on skis and delivery boys pulling sleds. Audrey Wood, fortunately, made sure this time that there was more than a pint of bourbon on the mantel. There had been, if I remember correctly, a fifth of bourbon and of rye for the forty-odd guests before she arrived and frantically ordered more liquor and hors d'oeuvres from a nearby caterer.

Tennessee was just as calm following the less successful opening of *Summer and Smoke,* directed by Margo Jones (who had directed the little-theater productions of *You Touched Me*). His confidence and humor intact, he even gave a "bad notice" party two weeks later and invited the critics who had given the play the two worst reviews. Moreover, he prepared for the pleasure of his guests. I was in Italy, but he wrote me: "A caterer came and served hot ham and turkey and champagne and whiskey. And I distributed gifts to all of the cast." He included in his letter an objective judgment of the faults and virtues of the production, as sure as ever of my sympathy and admiration for him and his work.

The change to hysteria was foreshadowed by the time of *The Rose Tattoo*. Once again, I was in Europe when the play opened. On my arrival in New York shortly afterward, Tennessee invited me to a matinée.

The two of us sat in a box with Gore Vidal's roommate, whom he had also invited. The performance, directed by Daniel Mann, with Tennessee's approval, was filled with the kind of gags Tennessee had fought to prevent Eddie Dowling from putting into *Menagerie* six years earlier. Gore's friend needled Tennessee throughout, asking, "Have you had any offers yet from Milton Berle?" Soon afterward, I heard from mutual acquaintances that Tennessee was upset because *I* had been needling him about *The Rose Tattoo*.

Two years later, when Tennessee was in New York for the rehearsals of *Camino Real,* we had a conversation that I recorded in my journal.

It took place at Fred Melton's. Divorced from his wife in Georgia, he had returned to New York with a friend and started a silkscreen wallpaper factory. He was living in a drab West Side tenement building, but in contrast, the room where we talked was papered with his Seed and Blossom design, which Cecil Beaton used as a background for his portraits of Marilyn Monroe.

"January 26, 1953. Saw Tennessee yesterday at Butch's. We were talking about the Hart Crane *Letters*. Tenn said that he found them different from what he had expected, stuffier and, even at the end, cheerful—not the letters of anyone who was unhappy or was going to commit suicide. I said I thought the letters from Mexico seemed distraught and that Crane had committed suicide because he couldn't face the prospect of having no money again.

"'Nonsense,' Tenn said. 'He had just inherited a legacy.'

"'But he was returning,' I reminded him, 'because a lawsuit against his father's estate had been started and was apt to cut off any income to him for years. And he had always been neurotic about money anyway.'

"'I don't think anyone is ever made unhappy because he doesn't have money,' Tenn said. 'I don't think having money or not having it has anything to do with happiness.'

"Butch said he didn't think that was so; hadn't Tenn been unhappy when he was poor? No, Tenn said; he hadn't minded it. Hadn't he minded being hungry? I asked him.

"'Of course I minded things like that,' he said, 'but I didn't think about them. I've been far more unhappy when I've had money than when I didn't. Not having money simply isn't important enough to think about.'"

I don't believe that, having money, Tennessee began to write to make money. But money was inextricably bound up with his problem.

As early as 1948 in Rome, he told me that despite the successes of *Menagerie* and *Streetcar,* he was not well off; he had only thirty thousand dollars: Audrey and Liebling had somehow diverted most of his royalties to themselves. However, even if he felt guilty about his affluence, he was happy and pleased with himself and his work that year in Italy. Shortly afterward, although he had just cavalierly impugned her honesty, he recommended Audrey Wood to me as the best possible agent for my first novel.

By the time of the mixed reviews of *Summer and Smoke* and *The Rose Tattoo,* Tennessee had acquired a taste for approval. Believing that both plays would have been commercially more successful, *and better,* if Kazan had directed them, he spent two years rewriting *Camino Real* in the hope of cinching Kazan as director.

After *Camino Real,* even though it was not the box-office hit he wanted, he did the same thing with *Cat on a Hot Tin Roof.*

His taste for approval had come to him with the one problem he couldn't solve:

". . . fame, that public destruction of one in the process of becoming, into whose building-ground the mob breaks, displacing his stones." (Rainer Maria Rilke)

Another parenthesis.

At the time he wrote *Cat on a Hot Tin Roof,* Tennessee was capable of writing as well as ever. He had recently published one of the most perfect stories I have read, "Three Players of a Summer Game," the short story *Cat* was adapted from.

It is not exceptional that the story and the drama are very different. Most of Tennessee's plays that sprang from his stories, and they are a majority, resulted from his compulsion to express his emotional material more fully, more exhaustively, the compulsion that made him write the stories themselves over and over, sometimes altering only nuances, sometimes creating virtually new works.

Only two characters are common to both "Three Players" and *Cat.* The subsidiary figures, the incidents, the dramatic viewpoint, are different. But the central situation is the same: Brick Pollitt feels that his self-respect has been taken away from him, sexually cut off by his wife, Margaret. Out of shame and disgust, he has stopped sleeping with her and has turned to drink.

In the story, at the center of Brick's "moral paralysis" is silence. "And then something must have happened that made no sound at all." Tennessee's language continually alternates the poetic and symbolic with the local and concrete. It pictures the events more than it narrates them, as though he is writing an account in words of a painting by Bonnard, weaving around the central silence "a snare for the truth of human experience."

Reading the play today, I find it easier than in 1955 to see what a successful dramatic conception it was based on. The language, considering the different requirements of the theater, is as skillful as in the story. At the same time, it is easier to see how aware Tennessee was that something unpropitious had happened to the script during the production.

In the printed version he expresses his awareness in a long stage direction in Act Two. This page-long interpolation reads like a disavowal of the theme that has replaced the silence, a plea to the director to restore the play's integrity.

"The bird that I hope to catch in the net of this play is not the solution of one man's psychological problem. I'm trying to catch the true quality of experience in a group of people, that cloudy, flickering, evanescent—fiercely charged!—interplay of live human beings in the thundercloud of a common crisis. Some mystery should be left. . . ."

In his hope of protecting both the play and himself, he adds a "Note of Explanation." In it he pretends that the flaws are only in the "Broadway version" of the third act, which he includes after the "original version." His guilt will not let him directly admit what he knows is true: that the character of Margaret, Maggie the Cat, has been fatally falsified. Her rich family has been replaced by a poor one to ameliorate her greed for money; her coldness replaced by coquetry. She has been sweetened to make her "more clearly sympathetic" and "charming" to the audience. And in the process Brick's "state of spiritual disrepair" has been turned upside down: it is no longer the result of Maggie's aggressiveness; it is the cause of it.

Faced with this incongruity, in the scene with his long, disavowing and pleading stage direction, Tennessee gave up. He replaced the "mystery . . . always left in the revelation of character in life, even in one's own character to himself" with "—sodomy!—." He sacrificed the mystery for a homosexuality that reduced rather than increased the honesty of the play, a fake homosexuality, suspected but nonexistent, a *Tea and Sympathy* homosexuality. And, as he habitually did when unable to admit his knowledge directly, he relieved his feelings in his work. When Brick shouts "—sodomy!—" and talks of "mendacity," Big Daddy mocks, "That half-ass story!" and "—crap—if you got to use that kind of language about a thing, it's ninety-proof bull, and I'm not buying any."

Tennessee Williams: Biloxi, 1946

Tennessee (in the early 1940s), with friends on Captain Jack's
Wharf in Provincetown, where he met Kip

On the beach, Provincetown, 1941

Tennessee, Marlon Brando and Jo Healy, 1947

In the *Dance Index* office, New York, 1943

Piazza di Santa Maria in Trastevere, Rome, May, 1948

"With love from Charlie J. Fatburger and friend," August, 1961

Truman and Sandy on the Kansas border, October, 1964
(Photograph by Alvin Dewey)

Tennessee and Don in Jack Dempsey's Bar, June, 1944

Tennessee and Don, Rome, 1948

· 8 ·

I went to the out-of-town opening of *Cat* in Philadelphia. At the intermission I ran into Tennessee in the bar next door to the theater. "Don't tell me what you think of the play," he called when he saw me; "I don't want to hear it now." After the performance, with Sandy and Melton, who had driven us down, I returned to New York without seeing Tennessee again. The next week, I heard that he was furious I had not spoken to him about the play.

I went to the New York opening. Sitting in the balcony, I saw Tennessee only at a distance. It was Audrey Wood whom he ran into in the alleyway after the performance, as he was fleeing the theater and, projecting his guilt, called a rat leaving a sinking ship. Soon afterward in a rational moment, he dedicated *Cat* to her. From then on, enigmatically, if, alas, typically, he distrusted her more and more. A few years later, he removed the dedication from the New Directions editions of the play. Eventually, he denounced her as having wished him dead for ten years and severed all relations between them.*

Along with a taste for approval, fame had brought him irreconcilable ambivalences of guilt and vanity. The problem is not new:

"Thirteen and a half years of success turned Alexander the Great into a kind of madman. Good fortune of exactly the same duration produced the same disorder in Napoleon." (Stendhal)

Thirteen and a half years after *Menagerie,* writing *Sweet Bird of Youth,* Tennessee dramatized himself in Princess Kosmonopolis as a "monster" and a "failure." Kosmonopolis mocks herself: "Mon-

---

*For a few years, the dedication page in the New Directions edition was blank. The last time I looked at a copy in a bookstore, it read "For Maria."

sters don't die early; they hang on long. Awfully long. Their vanity's infinite, almost as infinite as their disgust with themselves." She bemoans her fate: "After failure comes flight. Nothing ever comes after failure but flight."

But despite his self-dramatizing and his continuing transference of his self-judgments to people who cared for him and his writing as much as he himself did—it didn't work.

The year following the opening of *Sweet Bird,* Tennessee wrote me a letter about my novel *The Hero Continues.* After acknowledging that my effort to understand the character of the hero was more "merciful" than he would have expected if the book portrayed him, he refers to the hero as a "zombie." At the time, the word seemed to me a non sequitur. Whatever else the hero of the novel was—whatever his traits from the book mentioned by Tennessee, and those traits from Tennessee's own life not in the book but lent by him to the hero in his summary of it—the hero is not presented as a corpse endowed with a mechanical semblance of life. The idea of Tennessee as a zombie had never occurred to me. Only years later did I realize that by then Tennessee judged himself, in comparison to what he had been, a zombie, and assumed that, with my knowledge of him and what he tried to conceal, I must share this judgment.

He said that he was rewriting *Sweet Bird.* He was cutting out the "nonintegrated, barely even peripheral" scenes with which he had violated its integrity. Like *Cat,* it had been a box-office hit, playing nearly four hundred performances in New York; but he described it as "a play already produced and finished on Broadway and limping about the country on tour."

What would *Cat* and *Sweet Bird* have been like if Tennessee had not rewritten them for Broadway? What would *Suddenly Last Summer,* produced off-Broadway between them, have been like if he had? Two plays that are botched as art, and succeeded commercially on their subject matters and Kazan's theatrical presentations, might have been artistically integrated. One play that is a consummate work of art might have been botched. But the result for Tennessee would probably have been the same. He had lost his confidence.

. . .

Tennessee's personal life had changed by the 1950s. He was rich. For a long time, sex had no longer been for him solely a matter of vagrant promiscuity. After *Menagerie,* he had lived for a couple of years with Pancho Rodriguez, a volatile and poor young man of Mexican parentage. After *Summer and Smoke,* he began his life with Frank Merlo, who for the first time gave an orderly center to Tennessee's existence. He acquired apartments in New Orleans and New York, a house in Key West. His appearance metamorphosed from innocent to businesslike to natty. From 1945 on, he was repeatedly reassured professionally about his cardiac healthiness. But it had no effect on his belief in his impending demise from heart trouble. He simply had John Buchanan say to Alma Winemiller in *Summer and Smoke* the words he had been told by doctor after doctor:

"There's nothing wrong with your heart but a little functional disturbance, like I told you before."*

Of the misery and despair of Tennessee's life in his last decades, the humor gone, the laughter lost, there is no question. His manic grin of the 1970s, which superseded the upturned lips of his dazed, alcoholic beam of the 1960s, was further removed from his smile of the 1940s than that smile had been from the serious expression of his adolescence. Vulnerable, trying to protect his work with his confidence gone, he had lost his integrity. "Without it—what a grinning desolation!"†

The approach to this "stoned age" of liquor, drugs, and paranoia, to his "difficult, angry years," was gradual.

One day, a year or two following the success of *Menagerie,*

*There were, perhaps, other effects of this reassurance. It was in 1946 that Tennessee added a fatal cancer to his list of ills. All his accounts of his health are highly fanciful. There is no question but that he had four cataract operations, but his description of them in *Memoirs* has little relation to fact. Dr. Eleanor E. Faye, assistant and successor to Dr. Guernsey Frey, who performed three of the operations on Tennessee's cataract, annotated for me (she has recently performed two cataract operations on my eyes) Tennessee's "melodramatic account" (her phrase) of his vomiting during the operations, choking on the vomit and having no choice but to swallow it. "The eye was completely anesthetized and heavy sedation was administered. People were strapped down but were barely conscious of that. The vomiting could not have happened because the stomach is empty. They would not have continued surgery if a patient had vomited." Etc. She added that, although not certain, she did not believe the operation would have occurred before a class of students, as Tennessee said.
† *Letters*: page 93.

Tennessee came to a party at the apartment which Sandy Camp-bell and I shared. When Sandy brought him the gin and tonic he had asked for, Tennessee grabbed my drink out of my hand and cried, "I'll take this, you drink that one."

Peculiar social behavior, I thought; but no more, and peculiar social behavior was nothing new for Tennessee. Another year later, the three of us spent a happy six weeks in Rome together. That fall, Tennessee went out of his way, with the kind of outreaching concern which made me feel close to him, to help Sandy obtain the role of the young collector in *Streetcar*.

In the mid-1950s, Sandy and I were at Tennessee's and Frankie's apartment one evening. Frankie was mixing drinks and Sandy distributing them. When he handed Tennessee his, Tennessee sniffed it, muttered, "Poison," and, acting as if he were alone, poured the drink down the kitchen sink.

This was something more than peculiar social behavior. Nevertheless, Tennessee's and Frankie's life together went on as before.

By the 1960s, Tennessee habitually accused other people of behaving toward him as he behaved toward them.

Starting in the 1950s, he periodically avoided me and complained to mutual acquaintances that he was unhappy because I wouldn't see him. Then, if I called him, he would say he was just on his way to the airport or was leaving town the next day. "Let's see more of each other when I get back." And of course I learned, from the same people who told me that he wanted to see me, that he did not leave town at all.

As early as 1954, he confided to José Quintero (who expressed his concern to me) how unhappy he was because Frank Merlo—whose love for Tennessee probably withstood more tests than anyone else's—hated him. The reason Frankie hated him, Tennessee lamented, was that he had taken Frankie away from his simple life as a bricklayer and brought him into a world he had no place in. This was a foundationless fabrication. Frankie, with the Mediterranean heritage of his Sicilian family in New Jersey, and his wartime experiences in the Navy, was more sophisticated than Tennessee and had been, when they met, the lover of the composer John LaTouche.

These counterfeit accusations and complaints alternated with real kindnesses, I believe. The kindnesses I mean are not the known ones of his formal grants of money to writers through the Authors League. They are the ones that would have sprung from his quieter impulses, touched with affection and humor, as were his concerns for his grandfather and sister. They would have occurred in casual situations that were intimate and even nostalgic, that would have been expressions of the oneness with life I knew in him in the early years, and they would of necessity have been obscure and their own rewards.

The complaints and accusations were more obvious. In part this was because they were often preceded or followed by incongruous compliments and praise. Aware of this, in those middle years, when Tennessee did something noticeably nice I began to caution myself, "But what will he do next?" Not until the 1970s, aware that his kind actions were sometimes prompted by his guilt about his cruel ones, did I begin to ask myself instead, "But what has he just done?"

· 9 ·

A further parenthesis.

One day in December 1978, Burt Britton, of Books & Co., told me that Tennessee had been in the store recently and signed copies of his books. When he came to the *Letters,* he exclaimed, "This is such a beautiful book! I'm so glad Windham published it."

This was after Tennessee had threatened to sue me for having published the book. After he had denounced it in the *N. Y. Times.*

I was surprised, even if not as surprised as Britton. I asked myself, "But what had he just done?"

A few days later, I went to an off-off-Broadway revival of *You Touched Me.* At intermission, the director told me that the day of the first performance, Tennessee's current agent had telephoned with an ultimatum. The play could not open. Tennessee did not wish it done. Since the director had received permission to produce the play from the agent and had paid the fee, he refused to withdraw the production. He was warned that there must be no ads, no reviews, no publicity of any kind, no coupling of Tennessee's name and mine.

Three months later, contradictorily yet, alas, typically, the same agent telephoned me and asked if I was willing for there to be an all-star revival of *You Touched Me.* The production would open on the West Coast and come to an off-Broadway theater in New York.

One of the things that Tennessee had been "outraged" by in the *Letters* was that I had included a document in the form of a letter, purportedly written by me, that Audrey Wood had given me to sign in 1945, before the Broadway production of *You Touched Me,* changing the division of Tennessee's and my royalties from half and half to two-thirds and one-third. His indignation suggested that this was something I had fabricated.

At the time I was given it to sign, I believed that Audrey had prepared the document without Tennessee's knowledge. It made no difference that I could conjure up no advantage for her in the move, since she received ten percent of each of our royalties. I told myself that I was too innocent of the devious ways of the theater to understand her motives. When I saw Tennessee, I mentioned the letter to him. I said that I would sign it if he wanted me to, but that I thought he should know about it. He replied that he had not heard of the letter and would question Audrey. As neither of them ever again mentioned the letter to me, I believed I had been right.*

Two months after the agent's call about the all-star revival, five copies of the contract for the production arrived for my signatures. All the copies had already been signed at the end and initialed page by page by the producers—as well as by Tennessee. A Xerox of the original 1945 document changing Tennessee's and my shares of the royalties was toward the end of its sixteen pages. This page, like the others, had been initialed by the producers. Tennessee had failed to initial it and it alone.

*People who believe that this caused a breach between us do not understand.

· 10 ·

I saw Tennessee only a few times in his last years. But I can easily understand how his tragic quality attracted and enamored the people around him, just as his heroic quality had attracted and enamored me decades earlier.

Despite my experiences, I was moved when I read in *Memoirs* his words of regret that there was no longer any rapport between us. His making this statement in a book seemed to me to have more meaning than his complaints to mutual friends, which I had come to feel were meant as ends in themselves. With Frank Merlo dead and all contact between Tennessee and Audrey Wood ended, he was no longer in touch with anyone who had known him as well or had been as attached to him and his work for as long as I had.

When we reestablished contact and arranged the publication of his letters, the few meetings we had were pleasant. I did not foresee that the end result would be that he would again use me as a projection of his self-judgments and shift to me and the *Letters* his guilt for the unpleasant picture of himself he had presented in the *Memoirs*. But that happened very quickly. After the publication of the book, I never again saw him face to face.

Tennessee once said in an interview that at a certain date he ceased to lie. I interpret this as his way of admitting that at a certain point he ceased to be able to distinguish between truth and untruth. Certainly he showed no awareness of such a distinction in the various statements he made after the publication of the *Letters*. I began to fear him. I was even leery of seeing anyone who saw him. And if E. M. Forster is right when he says that fear, not hate, is the opposite of love, I began to feel the opposite of love for Tennessee. But I think that what he felt toward me at the end was something stronger. I think it was sheer terror at the image of himself that he had transferred to me and was trying to destroy through me, just as he had unsuccessfully tried to destroy it by transferring it to Frankie and Audrey and many others.

Our final, almost face-to-face, encounter took place a week before the New York opening of *Vieux Carré*.

For several days I had been preparing a complete set of photocopies of the originals of Tennessee's already published letters to me. Some were on dark-colored paper, or transparent paper written on both sides, and resisted ordinary methods of reproduction. But it was necessary for me to give a full set to the lawyers for CBS. Its publishing branch was planning to bring out a trade edition of the *Letters* and they had received the statement by Tennessee's lawyer that the letters, as they appeared in the limited edition, contained extensive and substantial additions and omissions, emendations and modifications, which altered their meanings. Tennessee had reread the letters shortly before they were printed and if he retained any distinction between truth and untruth, he knew that this accusation was untrue. But in the absence of evidence it was his word against mine. It had been made clear to me that if any letters were missing from the reproductions I submitted, this would be taken as evidence that these letters had, indeed, been falsified.

The completed set at last delivered, I went to join an Italian friend of mine, the writer Mario Soldati, who was in New York with his wife for a few days. They were staying at the Elysée, the hotel in which Tennessee kept a suite on the twelfth floor. When I arrived at Soldati's room to join him and his wife for dinner, he told me that earlier that afternoon in the hotel elevator he had encountered Tennessee, whom he had met years before in Italy. He had told Tennessee that he had just read the *Letters* and that the book was a masterpiece: an involuntary masterpiece, because the letters had not been written to be art, but a masterpiece nonetheless. Tennessee had looked at him, Mario said, in a manner that was mocking and provocative, and at the same time uneasy and timid. Then he burst out in a bitter laugh and said angrily, "Very involuntary!" and ended the conversation.

As we entered the crowded elevator on our way out to dinner, I was talking with Mario in Italian, concentrating and leaning toward him to catch his words. Before the elevator door closed, there was a commotion in the back. Tennessee, whom I hadn't seen, pushed his way to the front, attended by a six-foot blond stud. He exited, looking neither to left nor to right, as though this made him invisible and, followed slowly by his bewildered companion, went straight down the corridor until he reached a corner at the side of a door. He stood there, his face to the wall, ignoring the operator's statement from the suddenly silent elevator, "This is the fourth floor, Mr. Williams." Then the door closed and we descended to the lobby.

TWO

.

Migrations that must void the memory,
Inventions that cobblestone the
heart . . .

—Hart Crane, *The Bridge**

*Text of the first edition, The Black Sun Press, Paris, 1930.

· 11 ·

In 1958, reading Joseph Conrad's *Victory,* I copied out the following passage about the hero, noting that it was a perfect description of Tennessee when I met him.

"[He] was not conscious of either friends or of enemies. It was the very essence of his life to be a solitary achievement, accomplished not by hermitlike withdrawal with its silence and immobility, but by a system of restless wandering, by the detachment of an impermanent dweller amongst changing scenes. In this scheme he had perceived the means of passing through life without suffering and almost without a single care in the world—invulnerable because elusive."

In the summer of 1940, when I watched Tennessee's flight from Kip, I did not think of him as being unaware of friends or enemies; but I saw that he was addicted to his detached, vagabond existence. "Taking free conga lessons, working on a long, narrative poem, swimming every day, drinking every day, and fucking every night,"* he was happy in Provincetown. He was accessible. He no more intended to be emotionally pledged to Kip than he had been emotionally pledged to anyone since he had left home. Then he discovered that he was loved. Kip was not promiscuous; for him sex was not casual; his whole being needed to receive emotionally what he gave. Tennessee recognized the worth of the gift. He wanted to reciprocate. He tried; and from an overall view at the end of his life it is possible to see

*Letters: page 11. "Drinking every day" means drinking every evening. In the early 1940s Tennessee never drank while he was working. When he wrote later of having martinis sent up from room service while he was in Chicago in 1945, it was at the end of his day's work, to keep him going a while longer. In Rome in 1948, he did not drink in the daytime during the six weeks I was there, except wine at lunch, not even cocktails before dinner. And he worked every morning.

that what struck him to the heart was his discovery that he could not.

The extraordinary change that took place in Tennessee shortly before we met was that, as well as becoming one with life, he had become *one against the world.*

I think his affair with Kip was the first time since he had raised the solitary defense by which he was living that he was tempted to drop it. And he discovered that he could not break through the fortified shell of his ego. For the first time in his restless wanderings, he faced that even if he wished to give himself to another as an equal, to care as he had once cared for those close to him, the prospect was too frightening. Years later, the first of his books to be dedicated to anyone would be dedicated to the memory of Kip. Yet however passionate his pleasure and happiness were in those few weeks in Provincetown, they were not of a greater intensity, and they were of a lesser duration, than his pleasure and happiness in other love affairs. The importance of his romance with Kip lay in the fact that it revealed to him the price he had paid for the extraordinary change he had undergone. Unable to face it, he fled.

Reflexively, as was his habit, he dramatized his unfaceable self-knowledge; he projected it. In no time, it had become that Kip didn't care enough for him. Kip was interested in a girl at the other end of the wharf. Tennessee had been jealous of the girl, but jealousy was in no way an out of the everyday emotion for him. He was always jealous, even in casual friendships. He was transferring his unacceptable feelings into the other person. Kip was afraid of being homosexual; Kip didn't care enough for him. And in Tennessee's version from then on, no one would ever care enough to tempt him to drop his final defense. I think his affair with Kip was the last time that, still believing it possible, he tried.

Beneath his dramatization, he knew what the important thing had been. The affair marked an emotional milestone that he would not forget. And when he was at his typewriter the truth peeped out from behind the transference. "Breaking up with Kip," he wrote to Melton and me from Mexico, "was only an incident in a long cumulation of tensions and difficulties, actual and psychic, and the result was a sort of temporary obliteration of everything solid in me and all I thought of was my own immediate preservation through change, escape, travel, new scenes, new people."*

This description applies equally well to his departure two years earlier from St. Louis. As much as Tom Williams suffered from his personal tragedies, the outer events leading up to that departure were not extraordinary. Many a commonplace young man's story is equally dramatic. Without the importance lent to them by what came later, the most notable exception of Tennessee's St. Louis years is the length of time, in the Depression era, that he spent in various colleges. He entered the University of Missouri at Columbus in the fall of 1929, when he was eighteen. Three years later, his father forced him to leave college and go to work in the office of the International Shoe Company. But he had suffered a psychosomatic breakdown, his first recorded imaginary coronary, on the way home from a movie, quit the job, and enrolled at St. Louis's Washington University by 1936. A year later, his sister, Rose, suffered her final mental breakdown. Fleeing temporarily from this and other domestic turmoils, he left St. Louis and entered the University of Iowa. At twenty-six, his long adolescence was growing to an end. By the end of 1938, when he was twenty-seven, he had obtained his degree and his father had given an ultimatum for him to get a regular job. He responded by going to Chicago and applying to be taken on by the WPA Writers Project, a move he knew his family, especially his father, would consider a request for federal charity and a disgrace. Refused because of his family's affluence, he fled St. Louis permanently. He went to New Orleans. There he became Tennessee.†

The extraordinary change that took place in Tennessee—and that had surfaced sufficiently by the time we met for me to think that he must always have been as he was—was internal. Its flo-

---

*Tennessee's recollection in *Memoirs* of Kip's death in 1944 does not coincide with mine. He says that he received a telephone call from a woman who told him Kip had ten days to live. I am sure that it was not until he and I arrived at the hospital that he learned from Kip's wife that his operation for a brain tumor had been unsuccessful and that he was dying. On the way, Tennessee had bought the shantung robe he says he gave Kip. When we left, he brought it away with him; he told me he wasn't going to leave it for Kip's wife; and he wore it himself for the next couple of years.

†The summary of events in this chronology is secondhand and I cannot vouch for its accuracy.

rescence was the culmination of a long process. It must have begun as far back as the start of his puberty. Its seed was deeply sown. And its kernel will probably forever retain the "mystery . . . always left in the revelation of character in life, even in one's own character to himself." But clues of its nature appear in his conduct over the years.

Tennessee would say later that he grew aware of sex too early and too intensely; I believe that what he grew aware of, no earlier than most but too intensely to face without some defense, was the universal fact of being alone and mortal. He became aware of his mortality so dramatically, so egocentrically, that the certainty of his dying overshadowed his life. It became so real for him that, in a sense, it was the only reality. He and life were the same thing. And under the pressure of outer events, this reality made him skeptical of the pertinency of other people's lives, emotionally incapable of valuing anything that did not come out of himself.

This incapacity helped to obliterate the painfulness of his personal disasters: his sister's madness, his father's contempt. But he could not live with his sense of mortality without externalizing it. He could not listen to the beat of his heart without being aware that it would someday stop. The means by which he held this universal horror at bay, and which, strangely, made him feel something resembling joy, a sense of freedom from all responsibility, was his story to himself that he had a fatal heart disease.

Most likely this fable was not a conscious invention; not a lie; it was the dramatization of what he emotionally knew to be true. Rationally, he was aware that we are all born alone and all die alone. He did not tell himself that his mortality was the only mortality. As late as when he is putting together the *Memoirs*, he is reminding himself that, although his existence can "dissolve as lightly as the cinder dropped in a great fall of snow," he is "one among many of [his] kind." But he did not believe it emotionally. And for him only emotional belief was effective.

Part of the mechanism of his indulgent believing was to protect it by projecting around it related dramatizations, legends that he could, on the deepest level, either believe or not believe. Transferring his dramatization about himself, he came in time to identify with people he fantasized were ill or dying. He was drawn to women vulnerably crippled or paralyzed by strokes, Carson McCullers and Jane Bowles. He also began to fabricate compulsive stories that other people of whom he was fond had fatal illnesses. These fantasies were not generalized or vague. They were as specific as the fable of his own flawed heart. In the mid-1950s, when his feelings about me became ambivalent, he confided to a friend, with tears in his eyes, that I was losing my sight and would be totally blind within a year. But if he could either believe or not believe these fantasies about others, their dubiety, by their contrast, only verified the authenticity of the belief in his coronaries, his heart as big as a baby's head, which they surrounded and protected.

I think that by the time we met, and particularly after the summer with Kip, Tennessee's emotional separation had made the commitment between him and the rest of the world one-sided. Between him and everyone else there was on his part no longer any but a feigned emotional connection. For him it was always *as if.*

Ironically, this cleavage was not only unapparent, it gave birth to a charm, a sense of humor, a reaching out to others that was frequently irresistible. By the time we met, Tennessee's sense of separation had endowed him with the freedom from conventional restraints that people feel when they are in a foreign country. It had given him the ease travelers enjoy when their awareness that they have no permanent connection to the strangers they encounter enables them to behave with a boldness and confidence they could never achieve at home—a boldness Tennessee could never achieve in his years in St. Louis.

In the sharing of daily excitements and pleasures, in the give and take of facing daily depressions and troubles, he treated others with a seemingly boundless unreserve of friendliness. Nevertheless, the abstraction and unawareness he occasionally lapsed into in company was not as temporary and superficial as it seemed. It was a brief evincing of what was permanent on the bottom line of his emotional balance sheet. It was the other side of the coin of his gregariousness.

Because of his reaching out over this gulf with humor and charm, his ability to inspire others to commit themselves to him became one of his greatest assets. Not held back by the ordinary, egotistical cautions that make most people put up barriers against those near them, he displayed an unguarded air that bred in those who liked him a desire to protect him. They felt a need to match his openness, to defend his unworldliness. Without understanding why, person after person felt the longing to go further in commitment toward him, to give more. Person after person strove to make something less amorphous, more determinate, out of what they believed was the emotional commitment between themselves and him—without realizing that his emotions and commitments toward them were always *as if*.

Part of their deception came from the fact that the emotions and concerns he expressed were often real. But they were his reactions to the situations he saw people in, not to the people themselves. When he recognized in others feelings which he knew from himself, when he saw other people in situations that he had been in, or could imagine himself in, he responded with extraordinary concern and identification. But it was because he felt *as if* the other person was feeling what he had felt or would feel; it was because he projected his emotions into the other person, exactly as he projected his emotions into the characters of his stories and plays. His success as an artist and his failure in personal relations was that the one was as real to him as the other. And since it was not the individual he felt for, when the situation changed his sensitivity and kindness could be replaced by callousness and cruelty.

Over the years I asked myself, concerning Tennessee's statements about his health and the inner and outer circumstances of his life, "But does he himself believe them?" The nearest I came during his lifetime to a simple answer was "Yes—but." As far as I could see, he believed—as an actor believes who is playing a role to which he gives all his emotions and sincerity, who means every word and action to the extent of his ability; but who knows, without ever thinking of it, without ever *allowing* himself to think of it, that a time will come when the performance will be over and he will be outside the part, himself and alone.

I also asked myself if Tennessee believed in the *as if* of his emotions toward others in the same way that he did in his dramatizations about himself. Once again, "Yes"—being all he had, these emotions were as real as any alternative he could offer. "But"—on a deeper level and at the same time, he did not believe. In his heart of hearts he knew that his affection for others was a currency he could not redeem. Here, too, the play would end, he would be himself and alone, thinking only of his own immediate preservation. And this was his tragedy. He was aware, as of a memory from another life, of something different that had been; and from this awareness sprang the ambivalence that underlay his every attitude and statement, even those, and perhaps especially those, that at times seemed the most earnest, and that year after year left him knowing "hundreds more people" and feeling "more alone and more lost" than ever.*

How can a person entertain mutually exclusive beliefs at the same time? How can he simultaneously believe and not believe the same thing? I can only give Tennessee's answer in *The Roman Spring of Mrs. Stone*:

"Knowing does not need to be consciously knowing."

Letters: page 250.

· 12 ·

The fascinating thing about trying to understand the complicated aspects of Tennessee's character and to put into words the "occult reasons of his heart" is that he has already understood them and put them into words himself. Seldom in his interviews and essays. As a rule, he touches the truth only in his fiction and drama. But there was one notable exception, one occasion when he told a reporter a basic verity of his life.

It took place in the spring of 1945.

Tennessee was in a daze in the weeks after the opening of *Menagerie*. Faced with the deluge of praise, flattery and attention, he clung as closely as possible to his old pattern—or lack of pattern—of behavior; and he clung as closely to the company of the people he had frequented in recent years. Only with them did he feel at ease and confident of his bearings. He repeatedly turned up in the evening at my apartment alone or with one old acquaintance or another; several times each week for the month and a half he stayed in New York, we went to the theater together, or ate together with other friends,* and with his mother and grandfather while they were in town. Four weeks after the play opened, when he decided to have another eye operation, he asked me to accompany him to the hospital and stay until he came out of the operating room. That evening and for each of the six days he was there, with both eyes bandaged for four of them, I returned and read to him.† When he was released, we went together for a weekend at the home of Campbell's parents

---

*Mary Hunter, Margo Jones, Jane Lawrence, etc.
†The first evening, I found him nauseated after his dinner, which is perhaps the basis for his description of vomiting during his cataract operations, choking on the vomit and having no choice but to swallow it.

in New Jersey. The main change in his daily pattern was the time he spent being interviewed and photographed. But he made no new social liaisons in the world of success. He even managed to work. One of the few times I dropped in on him, rather than his dropping in on me, I found him working, as I wrote Sandy, "on a play about two sisters in the South."

In the weeks before and after the *Menagerie* opening, I was busy. My days were filled by appointments with printers and binders. I was trying to finish an issue of *Dance Index,* written by Robert Edmond Jones on Nijinsky, in time for the opening of the retrospective exhibition of Jones's stage designs at the Museum of Modern Art. When the exhibition opened the middle of April, Tennessee went to it with me and Fidelma Kirstein. Afterward, the three of us and Melton ate dinner with other friends. One afternoon, in a spare hour, I took the manuscript Tennessee had given me of *Menagerie* to a binder to have a slipcase made for it. Several evenings, he and I walked along the streets around Central Park until after midnight, discussing all that was happening. The closeness, the absence of any apparent barrier between him and me in those weeks, may help make clear why it was beyond my imagination that Tennessee could have been involved a few weeks earlier in the effort to reduce my royalties on *You Touched Me* in order to increase his. The two of us went together to Guthrie McClintic's office about its production. McClintic and Katharine Cornell had us to dinner at their house on Beekman Place. The closeness may perhaps also make clear what I and his other friends felt about the disconcerting statement attributed to Tennessee in the interview which came out in the *N. Y. Times* the middle of April.

"The real fact," he was quoted as saying, "is that no one means a great deal to me, anyway. I'm gregarious and like to be around people, but almost anybody will do. I'm rather selfish in picking my friends, anyway; that is I prefer people who can help me in some way or another, and most of my friendships are accidental."

Caught off his guard in those first bewildering days of fame, he had felt the need of a defense after which no one could censor him for not caring. But the statement was so contrary to his habitual reaching out across the gap between himself and others that only strangers could believe it. For myself and his other friends, the words simply could not mean what they said. And the statement was so isolated that even thirty years later, when I came across it again while I was editing the *Letters*, I retained my 1945 belief that the reporter had quoted him misleadingly.

As soon as the interview appeared, Tennessee retreated behind the excusing interpretations supplied by his friends.

"Jesus!" he exclaimed. "How could anybody believe I would say something like that?"

He retreated further when he entered the hospital four weeks after the opening. Bedridden, his eyes bandaged, he was, at least temporarily, the one in need. His greatest strength, the position he had depended on, had been that he was one against the world. With such an adversary, any defense had been permissible. Now the tables were turned. The world was on his side. But he had been wrong when he thought fame gave him a greater liberty for revelation rather than a greater cause for concealment. He needed to regroup his forces.

In a quiet way, the success of *Menagerie* was for Tennessee a repetition of his discovery that Kip loved him. The happiness of the people who had admired and liked him all along was in his eyes a claim on the currency of his affections that, in the latter case as in the former, he could not redeem even if he wanted to. Unable to respond with sincerity, he saw himself as a hypocrite and a dissembler. Once again, six weeks after the opening— exactly the duration of his affair with Kip—he fled. And once again to Mexico. But so quietly and unobtrusively that no parallel was apparent.

It is unimportant, if also typical, that by the time he wrote the essay about his sudden transition from obscurity to prominence, "The Catastrophe of Success," the period between the opening of *Menagerie* and his eye operation had grown from one month to three. The important thing is that by then he had projected his unacceptable feelings. As with Kip, he had transferred them. In the essay it had become his friends who he felt were lacking in sincerity and kindness, his friends whom he suspected of hypocrisy and dissimulation. He had not turned to them, he had stopped calling them and stopped seeing them. It had become a cynical feeling that there were no friends he knew or trusted sufficiently to turn to—rather than a guilty feeling that he had turned to them once more for his preservation, despite his knowing that, as individuals, they meant little to him—that he had recovered from in the hospital, while he was "withdrawn from the world behind a gauze mask."

This essay appeared before the opening of *Streetcar*. It was the first of the series in New York newspapers, written to establish a personal rapport with the public and critics, that were published before the premières of each of his subsequent plays. Reading these disarming pieces (collected in his book *Where I Live*) will perhaps help people who never knew Tennessee to understand the charm and reaching out with which he spellbound his friends. In article after article, the mesmerizing phrases, as skillful as in his best stories and plays, with which he makes his heart-barings intimate and emotional, are a counterpart to the unworldly and unguarded air of friendliness with which he committed his friends to him. But the reader, especially the biographer, who trusts these essays for factual information, or for the revelation of Tennessee's hidden emotions, is in for trouble.

For the expression of Tennessee's arcane feelings and occult self-knowledge, you must turn to his stories and plays. With the honesty that dramatization allowed him, he expressed his real emotions after *Menagerie* most clearly in "One Arm," a story he drafted following his summer with Kip but put into final form only when he returned to Mexico after "the catastrophe of success."

In his death-row cell, Oliver Winemiller, the one-armed hustler, says of the deluge of friendly letters he receives, "They're bills from people I owe. Not money, but feelings.

"I meant something very important to hundreds of people whose faces and names had slipped clean out my mind as soon as I left them. I feel as if I had run up a debt of some kind. Not money but feelings. I treated some of them badly. Went off without even so much as saying goodbye in spite of all their generosity to me and even took things which hadn't been given to me. I cannot imagine how some of these men could forgive me."

. . . .

The unlikely setting of the above passage is far from exceptional. As a rule, Tennessee's more revealing insights are the most disguised in their dramatization and clothed in the least likely characters. The few times he portrays a character that resembles himself outwardly, the surface traits are ones that others might easily record.

In "Rubio y Morena" the writer Kamrowski "was lonely and unsatisfied outside of his work. He was uniformly kind to everybody just because he found it easier to be that way, but he forgot nearly all of his social engagements, or if he happened to remember one while he was working, he would sigh, not very deeply, and go on working without even stopping to call on the phone and say, Excuse me, I'm working."

But, also in this story, which was finished contemporaneously with *Streetcar,* but may have been begun much earlier, there are echoes of Tennessee's discovery of being loved and being unable to reciprocate. For Kamrowski, the realization that he is loved is "a beam that shot into his heart and deprived that moonlike organ of all its shadows, exposing in brutal relief the barrenness of it the way that the moon's landscape, with the sun full on it, turns into a hard and flat disk whose light is borrowed. He could not endure it."

The truth is clothed in his recurring metaphor of light and dark. The discovery "broke finally all the way through the encrusted shell of his ego, which had never before been broken all the way through, and he was released. He was let out of the small but apparently rather light and comfortable room of his known self into a space that lacked the comfort of limits. He entered a space of bewildering dark and immensity, and yet not dark, of which light is really the darker side of the sphere. He was not at home in it. It gave him unbearable fright, and so he crawled back."

Tennessee's transference of his discovery that he was loved and could not respond in kind into his defense that he was not loved, that "he had never been able to believe that anybody sincerely cared much about him and perhaps no one did"—a transference trailed by guilty doubt—continued to surface in his work throughout the years.

Brick, in *Cat,* replies to Maggie's declaration, "I *do* love you, Brick, I *do!*":

"Wouldn't it be funny if that was true?"

Miriam, in *In the Bar of a Tokyo Hotel,* after the death of her husband, having just defended her indifference as a narrow circle of light that she has to stay inside to protect her existence, muses:

"It would be strange but possible if later I discovered that I cared for him deeply . . ."

·13·

Another parenthesis.

Mexico, in 1945 as in 1940, was only an interlude. Tennessee returned to New York in the fall for the Broadway production of *You Touched Me*. By the beginning of 1946, he was established in New Orleans, living with Pancho. This liaison was an antidote to the poison of success, not a further potion of it. Having concealed his feelings, on the one hand, in his essay and in his disingenuous statements, and having expressed them, on the other, in his fiction, he once more settled himself into an isolated existence—a sort of stationary, promiscuous vagabondage—with a lover who had no claim on him from the past and who, in truth, he took from a simple existence into a complex relationship he did not know how to cope with psychologically. This liaison furnished him with the comfort of limits; it helped him concentrate on his work despite the limitlessness of his new economic freedom, and at the same time it afforded him a continual stimulant as exciting as that of his nights on Ocean Street in wartime Jacksonville and on the blacked-out Palisades of Santa Monica.

My closest encounter with this came when Tennessee and Pancho had been living together a year and a half, long enough for Tennessee to finish *Streetcar*. I had quit my job at *Dance Index,* hoping to devote all my time to writing. A few months before, after reading my story, "The Starless Air," Tennessee had sent me three hundred dollars to help me out financially.* But I

---

*Having read exaggerated statements about Tennessee's financial help to me, I worked out, with Audrey Wood's help, the amount of the gifts he made me through her office and the Authors League Fund, all most generous and most appreciated. They extended from 1947 to 1949 and amounted to a sum total of $2,000.

had not seen him to talk to for a long while when he came to town in mid-May with Pancho for meetings about the production of *Streetcar* and checked into Audrey Wood's hotel, The Royalton.

From my journal: "May 31, 1947. Yesterday I met Tenn at the Algonquin for a drink. He was half an hour late, but I enjoyed talking to him. After an hour, just as we were leaving, Pancho arrived, very bright and loud—and friendly, I thought. Tenn apparently knew better. Pancho insisted we sit down and have another drink. Tenn said no, but Pancho forbade him to leave, saying he was going to pay for this one. I said I'd have a drink with him, as I thought a friendly attitude would make him feel secure, and I asked if he'd enjoyed the play Tenn said he'd been to. 'I haven't been to any play,' he replied. 'I've been in the room. You ought to see your room now, Mr. Williams. Maybe you two ought to go over and see it together. You're both writers, maybe you can both make a story out of it.'
    "Tenn asked for the check and Pancho shouted for the waiter to bring everyone's checks. 'We're the sugar daddies!' Then he asked me, 'Well, did you get another three hundred dollars out of Mr. Williams?' 'Pancho,' I said, 'you aren't jealous of me, are you?' 'Jealous of you,' he shouted. 'I think you and Sandy are two of the biggest whores who ever appeared on Broadway!' 'I haven't appeared on Broadway,' I said, still hoping to make him agreeable. Tenn, who was still standing up, disappeared behind a screen at the end of the lobby while Pancho continued about how low I was and how Tennessee supported everyone. When the waiter arrived, Tenn appeared and paid the check, left a dollar in change for the tip, and fled.
    "Pancho, without ceasing his monologue, dumped the change from the tray onto the table. 'Is this for me?' the waiter asked. 'No, that is for you,' Pancho said, pushing over a quarter and pocketing seventy-five cents. When I stood up and left, he followed me across the lobby to the door, talking to me from behind and as I reached the sidewalk I heard him back of me commanding me, or warning me, never again to call Tennessee while he was there."

The devastation Tennessee found in his room, a typewriter destroyed, clothes ripped to shreds, books torn up, vases and glasses smashed, is recorded in the book of his letters to me. Pancho's tenure, the use Tennessee made of him, consciously or unconsciously, was coming to an end. Tennessee severed all relations between them during the rehearsals of *Streetcar*. Pancho was not present for the opening of the play, or for the party the day after the blizzard. By the end of the year, Tennessee was packing to go to Europe alone, starting off on a new step in his progress of keeping himself invulnerable because elusive.

·14·

My awareness of Tennessee's psychological self-portraits in his fiction and dramas peaked when I reread *The Roman Spring of Mrs. Stone* a few years after its publication.

I went through the book, underlining passages relating to his knowledge of himself.

". . . when a man has an appointment with grandeur, he dares not stoop to comfort . . ."

"For such encounters Mrs. Stone had a stock phrase of evasion. How wonderful to see you, but I am just on my way to the airport! The other party might or might not believe her, it didn't matter, the important thing was that it released her with the utmost expedition."

"Who are these people 'who ever loved me?' cried Mrs. Stone. Can you mention some?"

"She knew it in her heart without consciously knowing it."

"She lived, now, in a world that was subject to worldly laws."

"Mrs. Stone, for some unfathomable reason, began to invent a lie about herself . . . that she was afflicted with a malignant growth, that she had undergone an operation for it, but that the growth had returned. She could not live long. . . . While she invented this lie about herself, Mrs. Stone felt something resembling joy, a sense of wild freedom. . . ."

"Mrs. Stone had long entertained the romantic notion that she would die early . . . but now . . . the idea of an early death was exposed as a mere conceit which fate had no intention of gratifying."

And nearly three dozen more passages throughout the book.

On my first reading, I had been upset by Tennessee's portrait of Italy. It had overshadowed the real contents of the novel. No hint remained of the appreciation of Rome he had felt in 1948; the Italians are no longer for him "such sweet people that I am afraid I shall become a sentimentalist about the human race." Instead of being always pleasant, "just as careless as birds, and as brainless, too," they are cold opportunists in a sordid whorehouse.

By the second time around, I saw that the novel has nothing to do with Italy. The setting is only a skillful bit of packaging. *Roman Spring* is Tennessee's self-examination in the face of his knowledge that he has acquired a taste for approval. It springs from his awareness that his standards have made an about-face. In it he looks harshly at a character who has ceased to be one with life and has become one with a world subject to worldly laws. His own solutions to the demands of this worldly world, and the consequences of those solutions, are the source of the novel's authentic emotions. *Roman Spring* is the first fruit of his new credo—"A failure reaches fewer people, and touches fewer, than does a play that succeeds"—which he was about to put into use with *The Rose Tattoo,* even though he was not to put it into words until the published version of *Cat.*

At the same time, *Roman Spring* is, in a deeper sense, Tennessee's expiatory dramatization of his relationship with Frank Merlo. The portrait of the Roman "marquetta," Paolo, who is out to take Mrs. Stone for her money and to humiliate her if he doesn't, is not even obliquely a portrait of Frankie. But, read in perspective, it is a release of what Tennessee felt Frankie *should* feel about him. The portrait of Paolo comes from Tennessee's guilty realization that, once more, he is making someone love him even though he no longer even considers the possibility of responding in kind. For him, lovers and whores, as well as friends and strangers, are the same.

The portrait also comes from his awareness that his new ménage, aside from its sexual intensity, is a part of his accommodation to the catastrophe of success, not an opposition to it as his liaison with Pancho had been. The portrait is a dramatization of his shame that this accommodation enables him with impunity to seem even more open and unguarded in the distribution of his emotional currency. It assuages his guilty knowledge—and at the same time prevents it from becoming conscious knowledge—that the day will come when he will be unable *not* to sacrifice Frankie to his own immediate preservation, or to his own momentary desires, for which he feels he deserves to be made to pay in pain and money, blackmail and humiliation.

On my first reading, I was also distracted from the real contents of the novel by other factors. Perhaps because it was written more quickly than any of his plays or even short stories—a year and a half from inception to publication—its sources are more evident.

The professional circumstances of Mrs. Stone are recognizably based on Tennessee's view of Katharine Cornell. At the time of *Menagerie* and *You Touched Me,* she and Guthrie McClintic had courted him to write a play for her, and while he was drafting the first version of *Streetcar* he considered submitting it to them. But before he finished the play he knew that she was wrong for Blanche. The subjective reason he latched on to was that she was too old. His face-to-face encounters with her had not lived up to his romantic memories from across the footlights and he repeatedly commented to me on how unfortunately she had aged.

Also, Tennessee had written me that his model for Mrs. Stone was Eyre de Lanux. Eyre, whom we had both met in Rome two years before, was an American painter and writer, then in her early fifties, handsomely beautiful. She had been married after the First World War to André Gide's secretary (and son of his music teacher) Pierre de Lanux, and lived in Paris throughout the twenties and thirties. The character of Mrs. Stone has no more resemblance to her than the character of Paolo has to Frankie. But Eyre did have a Roman friend named Paolo. And in Rome in 1948 Tennessee met him with her, as I did.

That year Tennessee was in his businesslike phase of appearance, but his table manners had not lost the crudeness they had possessed when I met him. He still chomped his food. When he ate spaghetti he smeared the sauce over the lower part of his face. One day in a restaurant at the end of via Margutta, Paolo, with Roman arrogance and the impatience of the father of an ill-trained child, took his napkin, reached across the table, and without so much as a by-your-leave wiped Tennessee's tomato-stained mouth. ("It was a reprisal for something a long time ago" is another sentence I underlined in the novel.)

The Paolo of the novel has no more resemblance to the Paolo of life than it has to Frankie; but in the novel Tennessee used details from unpublished stories by Eyre, based on childhood reminiscences told her by Paolo, which both he and I had read. He used, as well, circumstances of actual business transactions that Eyre had told him Paolo was involved in. All these things hindered me at first from seeing the novel as what it is; but on rereading I had no trouble in recognizing *Mrs. Stone,* the book, not just the character, as Tennessee's fictional self-portrait.

A journal entry from 1959, the time of *Sweet Bird:*

"January 30. Eyre to lunch yesterday. She told me the story of her running into Tennessee a year ago on the via Veneto. She greeted him friendlily, forgetting that she should not feel so, and they sat down to have a drink. After a while she said to him:

"'Tennessee, why did you do it?'

"'Do what?' he asked.

"When she told him what, he said that she didn't understand. Nobody understood.

"'All those people are me,' he said. 'Not you, not others. And the worse they are the more they are me. All I did was to use some little incidents and stories you had told me.'

"'But the name?' she asked. 'At least you could have changed the name.'

"'But I like the name Paolo, Eyre, darling. It's such a beautiful name.'"

Tennessee's dramatizations of himself as predatory females, which start in *The Roman Spring of Mrs. Stone,* herald a change in the nature of his writing.

In his early plays—and in the stories gathered in his first two collections, *One Arm* (1948) and *Hard Candy* (1954)—he projects his emotions equally into the assorted characters and events. The subject matter is his reaction to life, not merely to the characters and events through which he expresses it and gives it form.

(This is why it can be misleading to deduce real-life events from the "I" of a story like "The Resemblance Between a Violin Case and a Coffin," biographical facts from the Tom of *The Glass Menagerie:* the mask is on the observations when he designates himself, as it is on the characters in his self-portraits as vain and monstrous women.)*

In his writings in the 1950s his raw material begins to veer away from being an isolated individual's reaction to life and toward being an isolated individual's reaction to himself and his condition.

Throughout the decade, the mixture of these two kinds of writing is more or less even, six of one, half a dozen of the other. But the main characters are increasingly condemnatory self-portraits, the subsidiary characters increasingly one-dimensional clichés after *Sweet Bird of Youth,* in which the only developed characters, the Princess Kosmonopolis and Chance Wayne, are both self-portraits—each sharing Tennessee's trait of washing down pills with alcohol to control hysteria, each concentrating physically and emotionally on his own heart, each ruthlessly determined to have the spotlight on himself alone—to such a degree that they resemble egocentric Siamese twins cavorting before a distorting mirror.

*The sensual awareness, the lust, the shame of the narrator in the story are those of Tennessee's more mature self, as he parenthetically admits: "No, I am not putting all of these things in their exact chronological order." The circumstances of Tom in the play, and his character except when he speaks as narrator, are drawn more from the co-workers Tennessee observed in his job at the shoe company than from himself.

THREE

.

*"Society knows very well how
to go about suppressing a man and has
methods more subtle than death."*

—André Gide, "In Memoriam: Oscar
Wilde"

The years during which the nature of Tennessee's writing was changing were those when he was living with Frank Merlo.

Frankie, without question, gave an orderly center to Tennessee's existence. "He had a gift for creating a life" was Tennessee's way of putting it. But it required more than a gift; it required persistent hard work to create and perpetuate a social and emotional set-up that accommodated Tennessee's behavior throughout this period.

In his post-Frankie novel, *Moise and the World of Reason,* Tennessee's protagonist, his eccentric portrait of himself as a young writer, says to the subprotagonist, his straight portrait of himself as an aging, stumbling, drunken playwright, that he has encountered a word he didn't know before, "solipsism." It means, he explains, to live exclusively in and for yourself. He asks if he should write it down for the playwright, who replies, "I know the word as well as I know my name."

I, myself, recently encountered a word I wasn't familiar with, "palter": to act insincerely or deceitfully; equivocate, shift, play fast and loose, trifle.

For nearly fourteen years Frankie maintained a socially viable existence for Tennessee to survive in, despite the fact that Tennessee's method of remaining invulnerable, after he was no longer physically elusive, became a combination of solipsism and paltering.

My closest observation of what this was like for Frankie came when I spent ten days at Key West in the spring of 1953, shortly after the Broadway opening of *Camino Real.* Tennessee and I were going over the revisions I was making on my play

The Starless Air, which he had promised to direct at Joanna Albus's theater in Houston, Texas.

I arrived fighting off doubts about Tennessee's participation in the production. His commitment had been in question several times in the two months since the mid-February evening when I approached him after a runthrough of Kazan's production of *Camino.* The version of the play performed at the runthrough seemed to me a cluttered hodgepodge compared to the earlier published script I admired, *Ten Blocks on the Camino Real,* and the production seemed to add to the confusion. I did not say this to Tennessee, but remembering his recent complaints to me about Kazan's excessive demands for rewrites, and his repeated assertions that he wished he could direct his own plays, I asked if he would like to try his hand at directing with my play.

He agreed and everything except a date to start rehearsals was settled between him and Joanna. But at the same time I learned that he was telling a friend of his who worked for the Theatre Guild, which was also interested in the play, that he had no intention of directing it in Houston and was leaving for Europe immediately after the *Camino* opening. Questioned, he hedged and told me and my agent* that he would direct my play in Houston "if he could," a comedown from what he had said before.

The last of these changes had taken place at the time of *Camino's* opening in New York. Tennessee was optimistic that evening. Kazan was his talisman for success. Notwithstanding his claim soon afterward that this was, like every other important occasion, the most difficult of his life, Tennessee was expecting a triumph. In the bar next door to the theater, where I encountered him before the performance, he asked me to join him after the play and we would telephone Joanna in Houston and settle the date. But when I approached him later backstage where he was with a group of people, not planning flight but arranging transportation to the opening-night party, he sent me away, saying that after two years of work on *Camino* he was not

---

*Phyllis Anderson: she was as dedicated to her clients as Audrey Wood and, in her concern, even more personal. When I went to Key West shortly after this, she knew I was hard up and sent me, unasked, an advance of $200 so I wouldn't be financially embarrassed around Tennessee and Joanna. She died in 1956.

in a mood to think of anyone but himself. The last time I saw Frankie before Key West was as I was leaving the theater, and he called to me, "Hey, aren't you coming with us?"

When, a day later, Tennessee telephoned me, sounding more aware of his connection to other people than he had for a while, I felt sure that his call came after he had been reprimanded by Frankie. He said that he and Joanna had agreed on mid-April and invited me to come to Key West for a few days before we went together to Houston.

In Key West, Frankie was continually alert on two fronts; first, to protect Tennessee from others; second, to protect Tennessee and others from the *as if* facet of his vanity that made him promise to undertake engagements about which he could not, or would not, avoid playing fast and loose. While watchful on these lines of battle, Frankie tried to keep sufficient distance between himself and Tennessee not to be blamed for everything, and at the same time to stay close enough to observe his shifting moods and plans.

The first night, Frankie went into town after dinner to leave Tennessee and me free to work. But Tennessee's strongest reason for doing a thing was in order not to do something else. Left with me to work, he wanted to do anything else; his mind was miles away from the purpose I had come for, or at least as far away as the bars on Duval Street and what Frankie was up to. Then, a sailor friend of theirs dropped in; and because Tennessee didn't want to talk to him, he said to me, "Let's read the play aloud." We did. He made notes. And the sailor went to sleep in his chair.

After the first night, when Frankie went into town, Tennessee said that we should go with him. In town, Frankie would be unwilling to say what we should do; Tennessee would be unwilling for us to part. By default we would go to a movie in one of the two theaters on Duval Street. Once inside, Frankie and Tennessee would, separately and repeatedly, leave the theater—the management apparently accustomed to such conduct—to have a drink in one of the nearby bars. Finally, the movie would be declared dull. We would all go to a bar, where Frankie would be greeted by friends and Tennessee would order a different drink each time, following a martini with a scotch, the scotch with a bourbon and Coke, the bourbon and Coke with a double moscow mule.

Tennessee worked in the mornings. Frankie went to the beach. Now Tennessee decided that instead of working mornings he and I would go to the beach before lunch. Frankie was left with Grandfather, who was staying with them that spring. Then, since Frankie didn't eat lunch, Tennessee drove the rest of us into town to a restaurant. Grandfather's eyes were bad; he couldn't tell me, Tennessee and Frankie apart; and at the restaurant he would be grumpy because he was unable to distinguish the fried oysters, which he liked, from the fried potatoes, which he didn't. Tennessee patiently separated them for him. He was as placid with Grandfather as he was ruffled with Frankie. After lunch, when Grandfather got into the convertible and tried to sit down the wrong way, facing backward, Tennessee laughingly set him straight. Grandfather demanded exactly the amount of attention which helped Tennessee to concentrate better on himself. He was, in his way, perfect company for a solipsist who, despite all his transmutations, never wholly became more than vaguely aware of the difference between being alone and with others.

Frankie took care of all practical matters. The last few days in Key West gave me an idea of what hard work this was. Between the day Joanna arrived to join us and three days later, when she and I departed for Houston, Tennessee made these switches in plans.

He moved the date for starting rehearsals in Houston up a week, then back. He decided not to go to Houston with us but to go to New York to see changes in *Camino* and then join us. He agreed that we should all go to New York together, read actors for my play, and fly to Houston from there. He decided that Joanna and I should go to New York alone, select actors, and "do the first day or two of rehearsals" in Houston before he came.

The next day, he agreed we could not select the actors without him. We should all go to New York. We would leave the following morning on the eight-o'clock plane. Frankie would come as far as Miami, deposit Grandfather with friends, then return and close the house. Tickets were turned in, reservations cancelled. Tickets bought, reservations made. Agents and friends in New York alerted.

The following morning at seven, Tennessee said that he was remaining in Key West. Aside, he explained to me that he felt Joanna didn't want him to direct the play. Conversation was thin as he and Frankie drove us to the Key West airport. Before we left (for Miami, where we changed our tickets for ones to Houston), I said to him, "If you aren't coming to Houston, please let us know in time." Joanna seconded my request.

"I give you my word I'll be there," he replied, grinning, "—unless you don't want me."

I don't know what kind of conversations Tennessee and Frankie had in bed in the mornings while equivocations like these were going on. But I feel certain that when Tennessee called (from New Orleans) a week later, saying that he would arrive in Houston in a few hours, it must have been, as his earlier call in New York to invite me to Key West must also have been, after Frankie had told him that he couldn't continue to play fast and loose with people the way he was doing, that there was no reason for him to do anything he didn't want to, but that he had to tell people if he wouldn't.

And when Tennessee arrived in Houston I did catch a brief view of what the pattern of his mornings with Frankie must have been like.

Joanna, afraid that Tennessee wouldn't arrive, had kept secret any mention of his name, any hint that he might direct my play. No arrangements had been made for his accommodations. When she tried on three hours' notice to make a reservation for him at the Shamrock Hotel, it was filled with a medical convention. So the first night Tennessee shared my room.

There were two couches, made into beds at night, facing each other from opposite walls. Looking across at Tennessee the next morning, kept awake, as I had been on and off all night, by his snoring, I saw him open his eyes at six. Feeling around on his bedside table, he swallowed a Seconal with a whiskey chaser. Then he got up and closed the venetian blind. Back in bed he turned on his lamp, poured himself a half tumbler of whiskey, and read. A while later he turned off the lamp and went back to sleep. At nine-thirty, when he woke up again, we ordered coffee. Automatically, protectively, he said that he hadn't slept at all. A while later, when we were both working, he said that maybe he had slept more than he thought.

It had not occurred to me in Key West that Tennessee started his day with a sleeping pill and whiskey.* Despite spending the mornings with him, I was unaware of his new means of keeping himself invulnerable and narrowing his awareness to "the one big thing, which was work," for which the cracking of his knuckles or the music of a wind-up Victrola had once sufficed. I assumed that he retained the belief, which I shared, and which he had put into words a few years earlier, that it is a mistake for an artist to think that writing "is something to adopt *in the place of* actual living, without understanding that art is a by-product of existence." His vagueness was something I accepted as being a part of his character. When I discovered that he remembered in my script as many scenes that had never been in it as scenes that had, I credited my dismay to my awareness of how much I was counting on his participation in the production. Only later did I realize that the anomalous series of drinks I had seen him imbibe in Key West was his attempt to find a combination which, on top of the artificial state of removal he had been in all day, produced the effect of calm, or of excitement, that a simple drink had once given him. Frankie didn't come to Houston. Perhaps Tennessee didn't want him to come. Perhaps he was delighted to escape. And who knows, if he had come, whether it would have made any difference in the conflicts that sprang up as soon as rehearsals started?

Tennessee was an inspired, if unorthodox—and, in the situation, impossible—director. His method was to improvise as he went along, changing the script, scene by scene, and adding not only business but dialogue and new dramatic elements. In order to do this unhindered, he barred me from rehearsals. After the

---

*Even so, this is a long way from Tennessee's injecting himself with "speed" in the men's room of a theater where one of his plays was in rehearsal, as I was to learn he was doing in 1966. Up until 1953, I don't believe he ever went beyond swallowing a sleeping pill or a Benzedrine.

first reading, he said that he had a "superb idea" for the staging and didn't want me to see it until it was worked out. A few days later, I slipped in and saw what was going on. As I was determined to keep control of my script, there was a confrontation. Tennessee was furious; he accused me of being unreasonable and ungrateful, and he sent for his friend from the Theatre Guild to come to Houston and "be on his side."*

As unpleasant as the conflict was, it helped the production. By the time the play opened, the script was the best it had been. It was also tied up by the Theatre Guild with an option for a New York production to be directed by Tennessee, a production that, by then, there was scarce possibility would ever take place.

As a result, the Houston tryout failed to bring me the main thing I wanted; for I was financially insolvent and I was hoping for an outcome that would make me some money.

On the other hand, it brought Tennessee even more than he wanted; for although he was never to direct his own scripts on Broadway, in Houston he worked out the method by which he wrote his subsequent Broadway plays after the next one, from *Sweet Bird* to *The Milk Train Doesn't Stop Here Anymore,* trying out the rough drafts in regional theaters, directing them, polishing the scripts and adding scenes until they were ready for commercial productions and directors in New York.

---

*Paul Bigelow. It amused rather than annoyed Tennessee that Bigelow told people he ghostwrote Tennessee's plays for him—although Frankie had been furious about this in Key West. But as early as 1943 Tennessee had no illusions about Bigelow's veraciousness, which he describes (in the *Letters,* page 77) as resembling an innocuous-looking glass of water "turned five different colors when poured by a stage magician!" My 1943 letter to Tennessee about the listing of him as the sole author of *You Touched Me* (preserved in Texas) explains: "I just do not like to seem to be pulling a Bigelow when I tell people we did a play together. But as long as I'm not pulling a Bigelow it doesn't essentially matter."

· 16 ·

The years with Frank Merlo were also the years when Tennessee worked most with Elia Kazan.

Ironically, Frankie and Kazan were the two people who did most to help Tennessee undermine his art. They tried with all their skill, their love, their goodwill, to give him what he wanted; and only an opposition that forced him once more to become one against the world could have saved him from his growing taste for approval. No one but himself could have weaned him from that; and no friend or fellow worker could have disapproved of what he wanted, or failed to help him get it, and survived.

But Tennessee himself knew and disapproved of what he was doing, however much he denounced anyone else's disapproval. The resulting conflict gave birth to the proliferation of cruelty in his work that began in his next play, *Cat on a Hot Tin Roof*. In it almost every character is deliberately cruel to some other character to such a degree that the play gives the impression the author is enjoying their cruelty, that he is using them to express the impulses that have arisen from his own opposing emotions.

For almost a year after Houston, Tennessee was in Europe, working on projects to carry out with Kazan. I was in New York, trying to reconcile Tennessee's and the Theatre Guild's contrary demands for changes in the script of *The Starless Air*. We did not see each other. However, we were parts of each other's lives. By then the bond between us resembled a blood kinship that can contain the whole range of emotions but that emotions cannot cancel. I was determined never to be in Tennessee's power again, or even in a position where I wanted anything from him.

My frustration and anger lasted for months. But nothing between us had ended.

Early in the new year, he sent me a card from Key West: "Waiting for the 'sunshine of your smile.'"

Reconciled as well as I could be to the loss of the Theatre Guild's production of my play, I replied with a friendly letter.

He wrote back that he was glad to hear from me: *Frankie* had the impression that *I* thought he had let me down with the Guild.

An afternoon in mid-April, a year after my stay in Key West. I have telephoned Tennessee. He has asked me to the new apartment he and Frankie have rented in New York, over Johnny Nicholson's restaurant on East Fifty-eighth Street.

I arrive at two o'clock. Tennessee answers the door wearing only jockey shorts. He is sipping a drink and offers me one. When I refuse, he slips on an embroidered black and red robe and conducts me around the apartment. ("I bought this chair for only forty dollars, things are so cheap in New Orleans. This rug is from the old hotel in Saratoga.")

Showing no awareness of the parallel, he describes Kazan as doing to him, about the movie script he is writing from *27 Wagons Full of Cotton*, exactly what he has done to me about *The Starless Air*.

"Warners won't buy it unless Gadg approves of the script and he keeps objecting to something new, saying he doesn't like things which he suggested and I had to do to please him. He's become too conscious of his power. Everyone has to do everything to please him. I spent all last year writing a frog-gigging scene for the ending, because he suggested it, and he wrote back saying he liked everything except the frog-gigging scene."

After he shaves, he puts on a white shirt, carefully knots a striped silk necktie, and dons a dark-blue suit with a white handkerchief, folded as I watch, placed in the jacket breast pocket. I think he has an appointment, but he sits down and smokes a cigarette in his gold cigarette holder.

I ask where Frankie is.

"Who knows? He always goes out gallivanting with his friends in the afternoons."

As I am leaving, I meet Frankie in front of the building, arriving home, and ask how he is.

"Didn't Tennessee tell you?" I see his gums are bloody. "I've been through hell every day this week with the dentist."

A month later, Tennessee gave a large party at Nicholson's restaurant. It was there that José Quintero told me Tennessee had confided in him how unhappy he was because Frankie didn't love him.

That fall. Tennessee has invited Sandy and me for drinks at his apartment and dinner in the restaurant downstairs. No one answers the apartment door when we arrive. No one at Nicholson's knows if he plans to eat there or where he is. Sandy and I want a drink, but the restaurant has no liquor license. While we are waiting on the sidewalk, the manager comes out. Tennessee has telephoned. He is on his way.

He arrives half an hour late, his hair damp, as though he has just had a swim at the Y, and apologizes that he has been delayed by Audrey and Kazan. Hustled inside to a table, I suggest having a drink at the bar on the corner. Sandy asks if Tennessee has had one.

"Oh, yes. I've had two double moscow mules and three bourbons. I don't need to drink anymore. Oh! maybe you'd like a drink. Let's go upstairs."

At dinner, he talks obsessively of his difficulties with Kazan, sounding as though he hopes to be told that what he is doing is wrong and thus to shift the responsibility for his own doubts.

"I've spent the afternoon down on my knees to Gadg, trying to get him to direct my new play. Jesus, he's difficult! He just keeps saying he doesn't like the third act because the character in the play who interests him dies at the end of the second act."

Reassurances ameliorate his tone slightly.

"I don't know if one should listen to directors or not. None of them are good on scripts. A director should decide whether or not he wants to direct a script as the author wrote it, and that's all. The trouble is that we need them. They have some sort of uncanny perception as to whether or not a play has the certain quality it needs to appeal to a large public."

Christmas Eve. Tennessee and Maria Britneva are eating dinner at our apartment. We have met Maria, a young actress of Russian parentage brought up in England, the same year Tennessee did, 1948. We both like her. Accustomed to living by her wits, Maria knows how to charm. She is one of the few people who, with a combination of flattery and mockery, good humor and slyness, can sometimes cajole Tennessee into seeing his absurdities and dropping them. At the same time, she consolidates herself in his good will by mischievous endorsements of the desires he wants to be encouraged in. Tennessee, as his compulsion toward cruelty grows, makes increasing use of her badinage to hear his barbs safely expressed, especially toward Frankie. The original plan for this evening was for Frankie to cook an Italian dinner. On Maria's appearance from England, he has made himself scarce. Tennessee has had Maria telephone and say that they will eat at our apartment instead.

On their arrival, Tennessee grabs my drink, as is becoming his habit, and lets me make myself another.

Kazan has agreed to direct *Cat*, but Tennessee's ambivalent complaints persist. He says in sequence:

"I'm a selfish person. My talent has always been commercial. It gets harder as you go along, not easier. I've spent the afternoon down on my knees to Ben Gazzara, begging him to appear in my play."

Three months later, *Cat* opened in New York. I did not say anything against the play to Tennessee, but I became responsible for all the doubts he had expressed to me over the year. From this, not from anything that had happened before, a new distance sprang up between us. Our encounters tapered off. It was around this time that he told a friend I was losing my sight: I would be blind by the end of the year. And I began to wonder if his stories about Kazan's treatment of him were real or the product of his imagination.

·17·

*S*uddenly *Last Summer,* the play after *Cat,* was the last in which I think Tennessee's concentration controlled his subject matter as it had controlled the lyricism of *Menagerie* and the passion of *Streetcar.* It was, in any case, the last of his plays that he was not dissatisfied with, the last that he did not rewrite after it was produced in New York, the last about which he did not feel ambivalent.

When I saw it at a preview I telephoned him, despite our estrangement, and told him how moved I was. He was fulsome in his expression of gratitude ("Let's see more of each other when I get back to town!"); but with Tennessee fulsomeness was a sign that his feelings were matter-of-fact. He knew that *Suddenly Last Summer* was good. It was still *Cat* about which he wanted to be praised.

I had encountered the same attitude earlier. When *One Arm* was issued in a trade edition and reviewed, most critics treated the collection with contempt. ("Wears the scent of human garbage as if it were the latest Parisian perfume." *Time*) I wrote an article putting forth the excellence of the stories. When I couldn't get it published, I offered it to Tennessee. His eyes lit up with pleasure at my mention of an article defending his book; but his interest faded when he saw what it was. He knew the excellence of his stories. The book he wanted to hear me praise was *Roman Spring.*

Bad reviews of Tennessee's work were nothing new when he began to carry on about them in the 1960s. Despite *Menagerie*'s success, they started with it. ("A fuzzy haze of pretentious, sentimental, pseudo-poetic verbiage." *The Nation*) The one-act plays collected in *27 Wagons Full of Cotton* fared as badly as the book of short stories. ("To call these plays obscene would be a mistake. 'Sentimental' is better. . . . Why most of these sketches were cast in dramatic mold is not easy to discover." N. Y. Times) But opinions like these did not upset him; he saw them in the perspective of his own judgment.

The clue to understanding the change in his reaction to bad reviews lies in the way he carried on about his grief at his father's death, as he had not carried on at the deaths of his grandmother and grandfather. He did not need to protest his emotions for them. He knew he loved them—as he knew he didn't love his father. His protests were nearly always to deny what he knew to be true, to denounce the truth he did not know how to face. And his anger at the critics' harsh judgments of his work began when they coincided with his own.

Throughout the 1960s, his plays became more ordinary. He had learned from Kazan that subject matter is the clue to pleasing a large public. And as he depended more on subject matter, his ability to control the form of his work with his emotions declined.

The Milk Train Doesn't Stop Here Anymore is a déjà vu double self-portrait: a rich former actress, "a dying monster," who washes down pills with brandy twenty-four hours a day, and a poor young poet who wants something from her. It was written when Tennessee was, as he compulsively describes in *Memoirs*, sacrificing Frankie to his own momentary desires and using him in his own self-destruction, flaunting his promiscuity before Frankie when Frankie was dying of lung cancer, having the police throw him out of the house in Key West and refusing to see him in New York without the protection of Audrey Wood. The poet has been transformed since the short story "Man Bring This Up Road," into an Angel of Death. As in *Sweet Bird*, there are self-revelatory speeches: "When I was still meeting people, before they all seemed like the same person over and over, and I got tired of the—person." There is more deliberate cruelty than ever. In scene after scene Flora Goforth takes sadistic pleasure in withholding food from the hungry poet. But the accusatory and self-justifying tone is the same as in the story.

. . . everybody who knows me knows that I am colder-hearted than the gods of old Egypt!

Why?
I have no choice.
Why?
I've never had any choice. . . .

As the characters in his writing were turning into clichés, Tennessee himself was turning into the cliché of the artist who will do anything to please the public, who will destroy himself for acclaim. His desire to regain the mob's approval was transforming him from a prince back into a frog. He was becoming as conventionally ambitious, as conventionally vain, as conventionally selfish, as in his adolescence. Tragically alone, but a victim, not a hero.

· 18 ·

In the years before the publication of the *Letters* at the end of 1976, after which I officially became Tennessee's "enemy," mutual acquaintances continued to call me whenever they saw him. He had talked about how fond he was of me. They suggested that we all have dinner together. When I agreed, these invitations vanished into vagueness. The interventions of Tennessee's go-betweens were always full of contradictory and confusing elements, of escape loopholes.

At the end of 1969, through my agent, I was approached by Tennessee's agent (still Audrey Wood) and New Directions about the inclusion of *You Touched Me* in the first volume of Tennessee's collected plays. I don't know if Tennessee, who had been in the psychiatric division of Barnes Hospital in St. Louis that year, initiated this approach. I don't believe that it could have been undertaken without his approval. I was delighted. Nevertheless, I had been told by Tennessee that New Directions never paid him any royalties. I asked for an advance of one thousand dollars.

New Directions replied (through my agent) that the volume would consist of three plays. My share of the royalties, as co-author of one of them, would be ".008333%." If the entire edition sold out, my royalties would be "$62.40." They were willing to pay me one hundred dollars. I did not figure out how they arrived at these figures. I did, however, read in the accompanying letter that the royalties to be paid to Samuel French, the publisher of the acting edition of *You Touched Me,* for their permission to reprint it was twice the percentage I was to receive. I said that I wanted to be advanced more than one hundred dollars. This brought the reply from my agent: "I'm not sure we can get any more blood from this particular stone." Followed by silence.

The next June, in London, Maria Britneva, who was by then Lady St. Just—with a townhouse off Sloane Square—invited Sandy and me to dinner with Tennessee. It was the first full evening I had spent with him in five years. My last glimpse of him had been at a preview of *In the Bar of a Tokyo Hotel,* early in 1969, as Audrey Wood led him down the aisle to his seat, an unseeing smile on his face.

This evening he looked thin, healthy and sober. Maria went all out to please him. She gave the rest of us a good Russian dinner; but she gave him a special, separate menu, shrimp cocktail, sherbert and soufflé, since he didn't have an appetite "because of his health." (On arrival, explaining that he was not well, he asked, "Haven't you heard about my last year?" He also mentioned that he had just had a swim and a bite to eat.) Before dinner there was a bottle of Dubonnet exclusively for him—he said that he had had his "one drink of the day"—and a separate carafe of white wine for him at the meal.

Tennessee brought with him a twenty-year-old youth, proper and Ivy League in appearance. Introducing him, he announced that his companion was an epileptic. The youth's behavior was quiet and calm; but throughout the evening Tennessee watched him with a wicked smile, saying every now and then, "Look out! I think he's about to have a fit now!"

At dinner, Tennessee shook his head over Gore Vidal, who had written an article in *Esquire* that annoyed him.

"Gore's cold, cold. He has it up here," tapping his forehead, "but he has no heart."

Maria's husband was ill in bed. After dinner, she sent Tennessee upstairs to see him, asking him to help her persuade Lord St. Just to enter a hospital, which he was refusing to do. When Tennessee came back, she inquired what he had said.

"I told him not to do anything he didn't want to do."

"But, Tennessee, that's the opposite of what I asked you to do!"

"Well, darling, what else can you say to a man in that condition? He was shaking all over."

The evening went smoothly. No conversation occurred that

could not have taken place between people meeting for the first time. However, we were not people meeting for the first time. The silences, even the innocent remarks, were full of deceptions. Tennessee made no mention of the inclusion of *You Touched Me* in his collected plays. Although I had intended to bring it up, I was afraid to.

On my return to New York the same week, I found a letter from my agent. He said that Audrey had an offer for the film rights to *You Touched Me* (a perennial lure) and was unhappy that the play was not to be in the collected edition. It still could be. Had I had any second thoughts? I replied that I, too, was unhappy. I hoped the play would be included. But I did not think that a payment of one hundred dollars was a serious offer.

Five more years passed before I spent another full evening with Tennessee—or, rather, two evenings and a lunch in three days. We were arranging for the publication of his letters to me. The question of *You Touched Me* was again in my mind. Montgomery Clift's biographer had recently interviewed me. Before leaving, she had asked why, as Tennessee had told her when she interviewed him, I had forbidden all productions of *You Touched Me*. Knowing Tennessee's transferences, I checked with Samuel French. *You Touched Me*, indeed, was not available. It was no longer in print, no longer listed in their catalogue of all the plays published and controlled by them.

At lunch, as on the previous evening, the atmosphere was friendly. I decided to bring up the subject of *You Touched Me* in his collected plays. If there was any misunderstanding, I wanted to clear the air. But the moment I mentioned the play, Tennessee said that there had never been any question of its being included. It wasn't a good play. It wasn't his play. Contrary to his previous attitudes, it was all mine.

After the publication of the *Letters,* in one of the series of diatribes he wrote to the *N. Y. Times Book Review,* copies of which the editor gave me after I answered the final one, Tennessee made another about-face. It may have been true, he wrote, that I had the idea of dramatizing the D. H. Lawrence story, but it was equally true that "Donald's personal contribution to the adaptation is not hugely underestimated by the word minimal." Donald had not learned "to write dialogue that actors could comfortably employ on a professional stage or even an off-off one. . . . For this reason the gallant effort he may have made to produce dialogue for the stage resulted (I would scrupulously estimate) in no more than eight or ten lines."

These passages were dropped in the final letter; it limited itself to accusing me of criminal conduct, planned intrigue and ruthless exploitation. My explaining to him what I was asking his permission to do was presented as a deception by which I made a public exposure of his private letters against his will, my giving him another book of letters I had edited and annotated as an example of how I would edit and annotate his was presented as an assurance there would be no editing at all except by him, "leisurely," *after* the book was printed. But to me the greatest enormity was his depiction of the book, which I believe gives a picture of him more admirable and likable than his picture of himself in the *Memoirs,* as a paranoiac and savage attack that, in another of his dropped phrases, makes him appear as monstrous a villain as any that he could remember from the early days of silent films.

His attack on my motives and the book seemed to me singular and inexplicable. I had been out of his ambience too long to view his actions in perspective. I did not know if he would succeed, but I did not doubt that he meant to destroy me. Then, one week after his letter appeared in the *N. Y. Times,* he gave an interview to the New Orleans *Courier.* There he spoke as though his letter were a routine matter of no importance. He said that he couldn't help but love me. He could never hate me. He suspected we would "make up" and be friends again. Out of my depth, I felt that there was no longer a common ground for understanding between us. I began to fear him.

Since his death, as accounts of his dealings with others in the last decade of his life appear, I have realized that his attack on me was, indeed, not singular but ordinary. It was no longer merely Frank Merlo, Audrey Wood and me. Many others joined us—in time, his brother, nearly every one of his agents, producers, lovers and companions. But his letter put me officially in the category of his "enemies." Mutual acquaintances no longer telephoned after seeing him to invite me to dinner.

From that time on, I caught sight of Tennessee mainly in theater auditoriums at the performances of his plays. The first was hurrying down the aisle of the Morosco in a muskrat fur coat just before the curtain of the Broadway production of *The Eccentricities of a Nightingale.* When he had published this script ten years earlier, I had been sure as soon as I read it, not from privileged knowledge but from internal evidence and memory of his method of working at the time it was supposedly rewritten from the version of *Summer and Smoke* produced on Broadway, that it was an early draft and not a final revision. As much as his successive drafts of plays changed, they did not regress into less form and cohesion, away from pattern and concentration. And even at the time he published *Eccentricities,* Tennessee did not say outright, only strongly imply, that it was a later version. But by then the production and Broadway success of his work was more important to him than the writing and the play itself. *Eccentricities* was a script that had not had its chance in the win-all or lose-all roulette of Broadway. To get that, it had to be new.

At *Vieux Carré,* produced a year later at the St. James, I saw Tennessee, if I remember correctly, in what looked like a gorilla fur coat. Presumably this play was composed a decade or two later than *Eccentricities,* but it hardly seems to have been *written* at all. It is less a dramatization of the story that is its source, "The Angel in the Alcove," than a cannibalization. The dismembered limbs of the story and its autobiographical references are hung up for display to draw the crowd. The subject matter is adapted the way novels are adapted for the screen. The heart is missing, if the heart is the writing rather than the sentiment. Remembering how Tennessee wrote in the early days, it is hard to picture him having written it at all.

· 19 ·

When Tennessee died, none of the people who arranged his obsequies got in touch with me—despite the fact that they were friends who had known me as long as they had known Tennessee. In the weeks following his death, I spoke to no one who had been with him in the last years. And so I attended none of the four (two Roman Catholic, one Greek Orthodox, one Episcopal) funeral rites, or the various memorial services I read about in the newspapers, that his remains passed through in the nine days between his death in New York and his burial in St. Louis.

Nobody likes a loss. I had wanted Tennessee to remain what he was when we became friends: a writer dedicated to making his art the best he could, whether it had a market or not. His later friends wanted him to remain what he was when they became intimate with him: a celebrity and a commercial success. For each of us he was, in a different way, our romance. He wanted what they wanted; and so they won to the extent of retaining their contact with him. I lost; but I don't believe that I ceased to be aware of his feelings and problems, and of him as a friend, even when I was labeled his enemy.

I do not know if the other people who were close to him felt any need to find an answer to his contradictions and complications. And I cannot be sure if the answer I have found is any less subjective than one of his rationalizations, or if it has any meaning to anyone other than me. It was the contradictions and complications that created his work. The work is what will matter to most people. But to me the life matters as well. I cannot separate the life from the work that changed as it changed.

More than a year after Tennessee's death, going to Florida to visit Melton in Fort Lauderdale, I made a detour to Key West to see Tennessee's house again. There it was in the dusty Conch neighborhood I remembered, behind its low white picket fence. But now the paint was flaking from its white clapboard walls and faded red shutters; the bare rooms, visible through the windows from the porch, were emptied of all furniture and other possessions. A summer house, hibiscus, palms and a few other trees had been added in the front yard. But the real difference was in the side lot, which contained the studio where he wrote and which he had vacated, moving his work to the house, and given me on my visit in 1953. The open stretch of crab grass that had connected the studio to the sidewalkless street was replaced by a seven-foot-high fence. And behind the fence a fortress of towering vegetation, mangos, banyans, palms, cacti, dracaena, shut it and its swimming pool, new since my day, off from the outside world.

Tennessee's early unguardedness and his late barricaded isolation came from a common cause: the terror of existing alone in the universe. However exceptional its manifestations were in him, it is a terror we all share. Perhaps the defensiveness of his early humor, so sensitive to guilt that on hearing a dull line in a dull play it made him see a glaring resemblance between Swiss and swish, so insecure that it made him ready to duck the base surprises of fate at the slamming of a door, was not so different, after all, from his shutting himself off from the world in the last decades with alcohol and drugs.

When he was young and anyone spoke of trusting in providence, Tennessee would reply, "Providence is a town in Rhode Island." When he was old, he struck pious attitudes. But at the same time, his description of eternity changed from "something that goes on and on when life and death and time and everything else is all through with" to "that euphemism for lasting blackout."*

His contradictions and ambivalences made him, in a sense, universal. Each of his traits was balanced, like the evenly weighed pans of a scale, by its opposite. He was ordinary in Montaigne's sense: bashful and bold, chaste and lascivious, talkative and taciturn, tough and delicate, clever and stupid, surly

*Summer and Smoke and Moise and the World of Reason.

and affable, truthful and lying. It was because he vicariously felt whatever you felt, whoever you were, that he connected to people in life and in art.

I did not laugh when I learned of the grotesque manner of Tennessee's death. And yet I did not fail to think of how he would have laughed in his younger days at its incongruity. Perhaps my feelings were no longer close enough to need the distant view of comedy for relief; perhaps they were far enough removed from those we shared in youth to take the conventional view of tragedy. Perhaps they were somewhere in between. I like to think that they were near to what his would have been at the end, taking what comfort there was from each, even though in his last desolate wanderings, as though searching to discover where life had gone, he seemed to find comfort nowhere.

In a speech in *Milk Train,* the young poet describes how, at night, small animals snuggle close to each other for comfort, nudge each other with their heads and paws to be reassured against the unknown dangers that surround them, their loneliness, and their fear that in the unreliable shelter of their world they will fail to please whoever it is they are supposed to please. Tennessee and I drew close to each other in this way, figuratively, at a difficult point in our lives. If the important things of life exist in spirit, that closeness existed to the end.

Another French writer said of André Gide that his friends found, in his affection for them and their knowledge of him, the basis for a secondary friendship between themselves. That was true of Tennessee's friends in the early years. In the later ones, those who remained close to him often undertook the task of expressing his hostility toward those from whom he had withdrawn. But even then, a subsidiary bond was sometimes formed between the ones who were no longer in his good graces.

After the publication of the *Letters,* Audrey Wood and I were in contact more frequently than in the years before, drawn together by a tie that once would have seemed unlikely. She helped me gather material, especially the financial details, to answer a libelous article about my relationship with Tennessee. The last time I spoke to her, two weeks before the stroke that left her in a coma, she telephoned to thank me for having sent her the issue of the magazine that contained the court settlement. She was glad, she said, that I had pursued the matter and set the record straight.

Then she gave me her latest news of Tennessee. His current agent (they changed, but were all from the agency Audrey worked for) had returned the day before from being with Tennessee in Chicago. When Tennessee missed the plane because he was late, he said, "It's that Audrey Wood's fault. She's just sitting there hoping I'll miss it."

At least he continued to think of her. Perhaps, even if in the same way, he continued to think of me. Certainly, there has been scarcely a day in the last forty years that I have not thought of him. And there seems little chance that I will cease to think of him now.

New York, June 1984–April 1985

AFTERWORD

After I ceased to see Truman, his rejection of reality became even more complete. I do not believe that his dedication to Tennessee of *Music for Chameleons* brought about the closeness between them that he wanted; but if so, it did not satisfy him. In "Remembering Tennessee," an article he published in *Playboy* after Tennessee's death, the mélange of fantasy and appropriation that makes up his version of their relationship outdoes that of his description of Gide and Cocteau in Taormina and his "remembered" conversation with E. M. Forster on sex.

"I was 16 years old when I met him." (This would have been 1940, the year I met Tennessee—and eight years before Truman did.) "He was 13 years older than I was, a waiter at the Greenwich Village Café and a would-be playwright. We became great friends—it was really a sort of intellectual friendship, though people inevitably thought otherwise. In those early days, he used to give me all of his short, one-act plays to read, and we would act them out together. Gradually, over the years, we built up *The Glass Menagerie*. I would play the daughter."

When a memorial service for Truman in New York was announced after his death in 1984, I wanted to go. Then I began to hear from mutual acquaintances that they had received invitations and, thinking of how I had been omitted from the arrangements for Tennessee's funeral, I feared that I might not be welcome. I wanted, all the same, to remember Truman in some way, and when Sandy talked with Alvin and Marie Dewey in Kansas and they said they would like to see us while they were in New York for the memorial, we invited them to dinner afterward. In the afternoon they called and asked if they could bring Harper Lee, whom we didn't know but who had been Truman's friend since childhood and had accompanied him to Kansas when he was researching *In Cold Blood*.

I cooked chicken breasts baked in butter, an early favorite dish of Truman's to serve to guests because it didn't have to be timed but could be left in the oven as long as he wanted to go on drinking martinis. As the five of us sat down at the table, Sandy proposed a toast to Truman, adding with regret that it was five years since we had seen him. The Deweys, who had experienced no contretemps with Truman such as we had, and who were at a loss to understand why he had ceased to get in touch with them and did not respond to their efforts to get in touch with him, said that it was eight years since they had heard from him. And Harper Lee, of whose friendship with Truman I knew only that he had always spoken fondly of her and had dedicated *In Cold Blood* to her and Jack Dunphy, said quietly that she and Truman had not been in touch for fifteen years.

It has not lessened but augmented my failure to understand what happened with Truman to learn that our three diverse friendships with him ended in the same way.

Back in the sixteenth century, Montaigne warned of the difficulty of judging men's outer lives and discovering the inner springs that set them in motion. He concluded that it is an arduous and hazardous undertaking and he wished that fewer people would meddle with it.

And perhaps it is enough if I have managed to set down here where certain people were at a given time and what they did. Perhaps the hope of understanding is presumptuous; and in retrospect I wonder if I may not have come closer to the truth in my understanding that I do not understand what happened to Truman than in my arrival at a seemingly clear comprehension of Tennessee's character.

Nevertheless, for what it is worth, since "As if . . ." was written, the *Collected Stories* of Tennessee Williams has appeared; and in the biographical sketch by Tennessee printed as a preface, his version of his character is very close to mine—and even more final.

"To the world I give suspicion and resentment, mostly. I am not cold. I am never deliberately cruel. But after my morning's work, I have little to give but indifference to people. I try to excuse myself with the *pretense** that my work justifies this lack of caring much for almost everything else. Sometimes I crack through the emotional block. I touch, I embrace, I hold tight to a necessary companion. But the breakthrough is not long lasting. Morning returns, and only work matters again."

Fire Island, August 1986

*My italics.